MW01601854

Puppy Training the Perfect Goldendoodle

Take the Guesswork and Stress Out of Puppy Training! Learn About House, Crate, Leash & Recall Training, Separation Anxiety, Health and Breed History

Helen Sutherland

Copyright © 2024 by Helen Sutherland

All rights reserved.

No part of this book may be reproduced in any form or by any electronic or mechanical means, including information storage and retrieval systems, without written permission from the author, except for the use of brief quotations in a book review.

The content contained within this book may not be reproduced, duplicated or transmitted without direct written permission from the author or the publisher.

Under no circumstances will any blame or legal responsibility be held against the publisher, or author, for any damages, reparation, or monetary loss due to the information contained within this book. Either directly or indirectly. You are responsible for your own choices, actions, and results.

Legal Notice:

This book is copyright protected. This book is only for personal use. You cannot amend, distribute, sell, use, quote or paraphrase any part, or the content within this book, without the consent of the author or publisher.

Disclaimer Notice:

Please note the information contained within this document is for educational and entertainment purposes only. All effort has been executed to present accurate, up to date, and reliable, complete information. No warranties of any kind are declared or implied. Readers acknowledge that the author is not engaging in the rendering of legal, financial, medical or professional advice. The content within this book has been derived from various sources. Please consult a licensed professional before attempting any techniques outlined in this book.

By reading this document, the reader agrees that under no circumstances is the author responsible for any losses, direct or indirect, which are incurred as a result of the use of the information contained within this document, including, but not limited to, errors, omissions, or inaccuracies.

© Copyright Helen Sutherland 2024 - All rights reserved.

With love and thanks to Sarah, Kasia, Georgie, William and Ayda.

Contents

Introduction

It met my first Goldendoodle in a puppy training class around 2010 where there were, in fact, two of the mischievous pups making their first attempts at "sit", "stay" and "come". Bouncy and smiling, they stole the show.

We don't really know when the first of these magical dogs arrived in our world but it's generally agreed that is was somewhere around the mid 1990's, with the smaller sizes coming along a bit later. This doesn't mean that they don't have an illustrious history. Their 'parents' - the Poodle and the Golden Retriever - date back to the mid-1800's and possible the 1400's but more on this later!

The creation of the Goldendoodle, specifically, was not an accident. It was a deliberate crossbreed developed to harness specific traits from both the Golden Retriever and the Poodle. The aim was to create a dog with the friendly, outgoing nature and the intelligence of both breeds, along with the hypoallergenic coat of the Poodle. This crossbreeding was intended to produce a family-friendly pet that could also be suitable for people with allergies.

The concept of intentionally crossbreeding to achieve a mix of traits can be traced back to the Labradoodle, which was one of the first deliberately created hybrid breeds. The Labradoodle was bred in the 1980s by Wally Conron, who was working for the Royal Guide Dog Association of Australia at the time. He aimed to produce a hypoallergenic guide dog for a woman whose husband was allergic to most dogs, and the result was a successful cross between a Labrador Retriever and a Standard Poodle. The popularity and perceived benefits of the Labradoodle paved the way for other hybrid breeds, including the Goldendoodle.

Goldendoodle's are impossible not to love, and its not only because their coat doesn't end up all over your home. Who can resist that furry face - and their incredible eyes! Known for their low shedding, they are loving, loyal and intelligent. And on top of this they make great family dogs.

Like their Poodle ancestor they are also generally healthy but like any dog there are a few health issues to watch out for.

I know quite a few of these dogs today. My favourites are the ones who's parents are friends of mine, Ayda - a miniature puppy around a year old right now, Max, a Standard (from another puppy class) who's an old boy these days, and another Standard, Daisy, who won't get out of the sea when she's near a beach.

Ayda's owner describes her using the perfect Scottish term 'Gallus' - which means bold, daring and reckless. A suitable word to use for this unique pup, that not only describes what to expect, but that also highlights the breeds Scottish roots.

It is hard to fault Goldendoodles - and it will be impossible to ever imagine a life before they arrived into your home - and your heart.

But don't be fooled but how cute they are - they are a force of personality and impossible to ignore, and you will fall hopelessly in love.

The History of the Goldendoodle

We don't need to go back very far to find the beginnings of the Goldendoodle, but the lineage from which this cheeky and energetic dog comes goes back to ancient times.

It's useful to understand this history, because many of your Goldendoodles traits, from behavior to health, take root here. Unsurprisingly the parental lineage is rather impressive.

The Goldendoodle, a delightful crossbreed between the Golden Retriever and the Poodle, has captured the hearts of dog lovers worldwide with its affectionate nature, intelligence, and low (sometimes, but not always) shedding coat. The history of the Goldendoodle intertwines the histories of its parent breeds an, as we know, these dogs make great family pets and provide hours of laughter. They like to play, like their exercise but they might needs more attention paid to trainings like recall and separation anxiety.

Before we begin on their training journey we need to take a brief look at their history - the magnificent Golden Retriever and the amazing Poodle.

Before we do that, it is worth mentioning the other famous doodle, the Labradoodle. This relative is a cross between a labrador and, like our Goldendoodle, the majestic Poodle.

Although both of these doodles look very alike as puppies, they can be quite different as adults. When fully grown, Labradoodles tend to have thicker, shorter hair that comes in many colors including parti-colors that can feel quite coarse while the Golden-doodle tends to longer and softer hair (giving them their famous teddy bear look) which is usually golden, black or red.

In terms of temperament, both are very similar but Labradoodles tend to be calmer and more reserved, and often more prone to separation anxiety. The Labradoodle is also more focused which is one of the reasons they can also make good service dogs. Mean-while our Goldendoodles are more inclined to be people-pleasers and many love to show off. These traits along with their loving nature means they can make great therapy dogs.

This really doesn't do the Labradoodle full justice but we are here to learn about our the Goldendoodle, so let's take a look at their parental line.

The Poodle

Your Goldendoodle comes from the parental line that includes the Poodle (either first generation or longer). These are fascinating dogs with an incredibly long history.

The Poodle is a breed of water dog and, like your Goldendoodle is divided into four varieties based on size. We have the Standard

Poodle, Medium Poodle, Miniature Poodle and Toy Poodle. The Medium Poodle is not always recognised as a breed type.

Poodles are known for being one of the most intelligent of all dog breeds, their athleticism and their sociable nature and they make great companion dogs and this is one of the reasons that they became Circus dogs in France. It might also be one of the reason that your Goldendoodle likes to do tricks!

While either Germany and France are often cited as the original home of the Poodle, she is most likely to originate from Germany where the breed was known as Pudels (in France they were called a Caniche).

Like the Golden Retriever, the Standard Poodle, was used by fowl hunters to retrieve game from water (usually ducks). In fact, the name Pudel translates into the old German word that means "to splash". This means that when you hear that the Poodle is a hunting dog it is most likely referring to the Standard Poodle. It also explains why your Goldendoodle is more than likely to love the water and to swimming (but don't confuse loving water with loving a bath).

As you might be aware, Poodles are commonly associated with France, and this is because France fell in love with the Poodle in the mid-15th Century. Louis XV was known to be very fond of poodles and, later, in the late 1700's, King Louis XVI and his wife Marie Antoinette were known for keeping smaller poodles in Versailles. In fact, the French were so enamoured by their Poodle that it became the national dog breed of France.

It was here, and during the reign of King Louis XVI, that the French began to trim Poodles in more outlandish styles and when they became fashionable with the aristocracy. It was also when the art of Poodle trimming emerged with the first professional canine stylists.

It was also around this time that our smaller sized-Poodles are said to have been introduced. Miniatures and Toys were bred as companion dogs and 'sleeve' dogs for Princesses and women of the court. Although bred to be smaller, it might have been a little later that we started to see the Miniature and Toy as recognized breeds. This is because Poodles worked in the traveling circus' in France, where they were clipped to match the pom poms on the clown's outfits and it is here, in the 1800's, that smaller sized Poodles started to become popular. This was for a good reason. The smaller dogs not only made great companions for life on the road, but the smaller size made it easier to travel.

During this time, the Standard Poodle remained a vital military dog – sniffing for explosives and hunting and guarding the enemy. Their intelligence, trainability, loyalty, and athleticism were perfect for this role.

So much so, that a black Poodle called Moustache became famous for serving in both the French Revolutionary and Napoleonic Wars in the early 1800s, fighting with Napoleon Bonaparte's army eventually being awarded a bravery medal.

By the mid- 1800s, breeders began importing Poodles to the USA, and in 1887 the AKA recognised the Poodle as a Standard Breed and classified it in the non-sporting group. I can't help feeling this should have been a controversial decision, given the history of the breed, particularly the Standard Poodle.

After falling out of fashion for a while, by 1961 the Poodle had become the most popular dog breed in the US, and it held the top spot until 1983 remaining in the Top 10 ever since.

After centuries, these dogs were eventually able to return to their hunting roots and are now competing in AKC retriever hunting tests and AKC Spaniel hunt tests.

They are excellent service dogs working as guide dogs for the blind, hearing dogs, and service dogs for mobility assistance.

In terms of their famous coast, it is commonly believed that the Poodle does not shed but in fact they do. Rather than the fur coming off the dog it gets tangled up in the surrounding hair and this is what leads to matting without proper care. This will become a familiar experience for you if you have a 'non-shedding' Goldendoodle and it means that his hair will matt easily so you need to pay more attention to his grooming than you would a shedding dog or shedding Goldendoodle.

Poodles are one of the very best family dogs that anyone could hope to wish for. Until, of course, we meet the Golden Retriever

The Golden Retriever

I need to confess that I love these dogs. I grew up with a black flat coat retriever called Paddy - who shares the original Scottish ancestry of the Goldendoodle (more on this soon). When the first Golden Retriever was shown at the Crystal Palace dog show in 1908, they were called 'Flat Coats". My beloved Paddy was originally bred for similar purposes as the Golden, such as retrieving waterfowl during hunting expeditions and their shared ancestors include the Newfoundland, the St. John's Water Dog and various spaniel breeds.

Paddy was the perfect family dog, especially with young children like us, who dressed him up and played with him constantly from the age of 2 to 15. Next door to us were two Golden's owned by a couple who fought in the French Resistance during the war - these two calm, loyal and beautiful dogs were called Penny and Tuppence and they were more than happy to patiently let us dress them up too.

The roots of the Golden Retriever can be traced back to the mid-19th century in the Scottish Highlands when the need for a proficient hunting and retrieving dog arose because of the growing popularity of waterfowl hunting in the region. Scottish aristocrats and gamekeepers began a quest to create the ultimate hunting companion, blending several breeds like the Yellow Retriever, the Tweed Water Spaniel, and the Bloodhound.

One of the most significant figures in the breed's history is Sir Dudley Marjoribanks, later known as Lord Tweedmouth. In the mid-1800s, Lord Tweedmouth began a breeding program at his estate, Guisachan, in the Highland village of Tomich, near Inverness.

He crossed a yellow-colored Retriever, named Nous, with a Tweed Water Spaniel named Belle. This union resulted in a litter of either three or four yellow puppies (depending on which history book your read), but it was this small family that laid the foundation for the development of the Golden Retriever breed we know today. Three of the puppies were called Primrose, Cowslip, and Crocus - incase you are trying to think of a name for your Goldendoodle!

Even today, and around every five years, owners, along with their dogs, travel to the 'ancestral home' at Guisachan in the Highlands to celebrate the anniversary of the breed's founding, in fact, in 2023 it had its biggest gathering to-date.

But, back to the history. By the late 1800s and early 1900s, the breed's distinctive characteristics, including its golden coat, friendly temperament, and impressive retrieving skills, were becoming established, and by 1903 the breed was officially recognised as the Golden Retriever by the Kennel Club (UK).

The Golden Retriever's popularity soon crossed borders, and in the early 20th century, the breed made its way to North America. The first Golden Retriever was registered with the American Kennel Club (AKC) in 1925 where his friendly and gentle nature quickly endeared him to families from coast-to-coast, cementing his position as a beloved companion dog.

By the time of the two World Wars, the Golden Retriever's intelligence, obedience, and willingness to work led to his involvement in various roles. The breed was used as a search and rescue dog, messenger dog, and even in some cases, as a therapy dog for wounded soldiers.

Their loyalty and dedication in these challenging times further reinforced the reputation of the breed as a remarkable and versatile dog. Today, they remain one of the most popular seeing-eye dogs after taking over this role from the German Shepherd.

Its good to know about a bit about the characteristic of these two dogs because you will recognise many of these in your Goldendoodle.

As we go on to describe some of the characteristics then training needs, remember that these caring and loving dogs will give of themselves every day - they will love you to the end of the world and back and you will feel the same way about them!

Size, Types and Characteristics

Characteristics

Goldendoodles are outgoing, trustworthy, and eager-to-please family dogs, with a joyous and playful approach to life, often maintaining this puppyish behavior into adulthood. This is the trait that I think of most when I think about Goldendoodles - fun!

Unsurprisingly, the character of your Goldendoodle comes from their wonderful breed history. This brings out the best in them but there are also a few things to bear in mind.

Poodles and Golden's are great family dogs and exceptional companion dogs, and they tend to have a long life - anything up to 12-14 years or more.

They are great with children and other pets although they are quite active with a tendency for hyper activity which means that they need lots of exercise - expect any or all of this with your Goldendoodle.

They can also be timid, and this can border on the neurotic, although this tends to be more common (but still unusual) in the smaller Doodle (and Poodle). Bear in mind that, as puppies, they can get over-excited.

They can be highly attuned to our body language and to how we feel - they can be very empathetic and, of course they have strong loyalty tendencies which can make them promo to separation anxiety as well as bearing the signs of the Golden's 'velcro' tendencies.

They can also have fragile egos so you might find that they can also go in a huff - this is something you may well see in your Golden-doodle! And, like elephants, they can have a long memory and really don't like being scolded.

Bear in mind that both Poodles and Golden Retrievers were once hunting dogs which means that they do need exercise and both are very easy to train due to their intelligence.

The combination of intelligence and high energy means that Gold-endoodle's need trained from the very beginning and respond best to positive reinforcement - with lots of exercise and lots of games.

Both the Standard Poodle and the Golden Retriever are energetic, powerful hunting dogs that love outdoor play and, as we know, were built to retrieve waterfowl. It means they are often that are great swimmers which means that your Doodle will love to swim (but not as much as the Labradoodle).

Meanwhile, smaller poodles can be protective which can make them aggressive to people or dogs outside of their immediate family, and they can easily develop bad habits such as nuisance barking. With this in mind, especially if you have the smaller type of Doodle, you will want to encourage early socialisation and training so that they get used to meeting new people and pets. Although this trait is rare, it's not unusual.

Golden Retrievers are slightly more likely to fear other dogs or humans so once again, early socialisation is key for your Goldendoodle.

Goldendoodles love to play and they love attention. Early games such as hide-and-seek, run-around, find the ball, catch, and of course fetch and so on. These games are also great during training. Don't forget to switch up the games as they get older.

And, don't forget their Circus background too, so teach them tricks - roll-over, sit-up - and get more adventurous. They will learn fast but if the stronger gene is the Poodle, they might like to solve a problem independently, so this is trait to judge for yourselves with your Goldendoodle.

Introducing the generations and Types

The first crosses between Golden Retrievers and Poodles were known as "Golden Poos" or "Groodles" and the early attempts varied in their success, with breeders on-going efforts to refine desired traits.

Over time, breeders and enthusiasts formed organisations to promote responsible breeding practices and encourage the breed's development. The Goldendoodle Association of North America (GANA) and the International Designer Canine Registry (IDCR) are just two of the best known and which have played a central role in the breeds development and standardisation.

The F1 Generation: Golden Retriever x Poodle

The F1, or first-generation Goldendoodle, is the result of breeding a purebred Golden Retriever with a purebred Poodle. Goldendoodles from this pairing can display a variety of coat types and temperaments, largely depending on which breed's genes are more dominant and the size of the Poodle used (standard, miniature, or toy).

Coat Types and Shedding

The F1 Goldendoodle's coat can range from curly to wavy or even straight. If the Golden Retriever genes are dominant, the coat will likely shed. This is important for those seeking a low-shedding or hypoallergenic dog—F1 Goldendoodles may not meet that requirement. If a non-shedding coat is a priority, you might want to consider an F1B, F2, F2B, or Multigenerational Goldendoodle, which have a higher Poodle genetic influence, leading to a more predictable, often non-shedding coat.

Regardless of the coat type, whether curly, wavy, or straight, the Goldendoodle's coat will require regular grooming. Their fur can grow between 3 to 5 inches long and needs at least weekly brushing to prevent matting. For curly-coated varieties, more frequent grooming may be necessary, as their curls can trap dirt and debris.

What is an F1B Goldendoodle?

An F1B is the result of breeding an F1 Goldendoodle back to either a purebred Poodle (most common) or a purebred Golden Retriever. The "B" stands for "backcross," meaning a return to one of the original breeds. When bred back to a Poodle, the F1B is more likely to have a coat that sheds less and is better suited for families with mild to moderate allergies. However, F1B Goldendoodles with more Golden Retriever genes (when backcrossed to a Retriever) may still shed and may not be ideal for allergy sufferers.

Allergies and Coat Maintenance

If you're concerned about allergies, an F1 Goldendoodle might not be the best choice. Since F1s are 50% Golden Retriever and 50% Poodle, they can be either light or heavy shedders, making them less predictable in terms of being hypoallergenic. Even an F1B, depending on the specific genetic makeup, may still pose allergy concerns, though the likelihood of shedding and allergen exposure decreases when backcrossed to a Poodle.

The F2 Generations: F1 Goldendoodle x F1 Goldendoodle

As breeders continued to develop the Goldendoodle, their goal was to enhance specific traits such as coat consistency and hypoallergenic qualities. However, with the F2 generation (the result of breeding two F1 Goldendoodles together), these characteristics can still be highly variable.

Coat Types and Shedding

F2 Goldendoodles can have curly, wavy, or straight coats, depending on which genes are more dominant. Shedding is equally unpredictable, and only about 25% of F2 Goldendoodles will be non-shedders, making this generation less reliable for families seeking a hypoallergenic pet. In fact, because of how genetics work, you could even end up with an F2 Goldendoodle that closely resembles either a full Poodle or a full Golden Retriever, despite being a crossbreed.

Why F2 Goldendoodles May Not Be Ideal for Allergy Sufferers

Due to their genetic makeup, F2 Goldendoodles can range from heavy shedders to light shedders, making them difficult to recommend for families with moderate to severe allergies.

While some F2 Goldendoodles may shed less, many will still shed considerably, and their hypoallergenic properties are less consistent compared to later generations or the F1B (which is backcrossed to a Poodle).

What is the Difference Between F2 and F2B?

The F2 generation refers specifically to a cross between two F1 Goldendoodles. On the other hand, an F2B Goldendoodle is created by breeding an F2 back to either a Poodle or a Golden Retriever. This backcrossing (indicated by the "B") increases the chances of the offspring having a more consistent coat, especially when bred back to a Poodle, which makes them more likely to be hypoallergenic and low-shedding.

Coat Care

Like other generations, F2 Goldendoodles require regular grooming, and weekly brushing is essential to avoid tangling and matting. Curly coats, in particular, may need more frequent care. Professional grooming every few months is often recommended to maintain their coat and reduce shedding.

- **Is an F2 Goldendoodle hypoallergenic?**

No, F2 Goldendoodles are generally not considered hypoallergenic. Only about 25% of F2s will be non-shedding, and there is a chance you could even end up with a dog that sheds as much as a Golden Retriever. If shedding is a concern, it's better to look for an F2B or a later-generation Goldendoodle with more Poodle influence.

- **Is an F2 Goldendoodle good for families with allergies?**

F2 Goldendoodles offer a range of possibilities in terms of coat and temperament, but their unpredictability in shedding and allergen exposure makes them less ideal for families with allergy concerns.

If you need a hypoallergenic dog, consider an F2B or a Multigenerational Goldendoodle with a higher Poodle percentage.

If hypoallergenic qualities and reduced shedding are important to you, an F1B or F2B Goldendoodle, which has been backcrossed to a Poodle, would be a better option. These dogs are more likely to have non-shedding coats and are better suited for families with allergies due to the higher percentage of Poodle genetics

Strange as it may seem, you can even find yourself with either full poodles or full golden retrievers with this cross (because of the way genetics work).

F3 and F4 Generations: Multigen

The breed's multigenerational lines, such as F3, F4, emerged as breeders aimed to solidify the desired traits consistently. The multigenerational Goldendoodles, often referred to as "Multigen" or "Multigens," have a higher predictability of traits, including size, coat type, and temperament.

GANA™ define a mutigen as two Goldendoodle parents where one parent has to be an F1B or multigen. A Poodle or a Golden Retriever bred to a multigen Goldendoodle also constitutes a multigen.

These types have become increasingly popular as they combine the best attributes of both parent breeds.

F3 and F4 (Multigen) Goldendoodles: Consistent and Focused on Poodle Traits

By the time breeders reach the F3 and F4 generations (Multigen), Goldendoodles have been selectively bred for specific traits, making them more consistent in both appearance and personality. These dogs tend to have a higher percentage of Poodle genetics, leading to more Poodle-like behavior.

- **Personality Traits**

Multigen Goldendoodles are often described as intelligent, active, and friendly, with more consistent temperaments than earlier generations. They typically have the playfulness of a Poodle combined with the affectionate nature of a Golden Retriever, though they can be more reserved or independent due to their higher Poodle influence.

- **Energy Levels**

Multigen Goldendoodles tend to have moderate to high energy levels, especially if they have more Poodle genetics. They require regular exercise and mental stimulation to prevent boredom. These dogs are well-suited for active families or individuals who can engage them in activities like agility training, fetch, or long walks.

- **Training Needs**

Due to their intelligence, Multigen Goldendoodles are usually quick learners and can excel in advanced obedience training or dog sports. However, their high intelligence also means they need constant mental stimulation, and they can become bored easily if not challenged. They benefit from ongoing training and enrichment activities.

- **Best for**

Multigen Goldendoodles are ideal for families or individuals who lead active lifestyles and can provide consistent training and exercise. They do best in homes with space to roam and play, though they can adapt to apartment living if they get enough physical and mental stimulation.

Key Differences Between Generations

Temperament Predictability

F1 and Multigen Goldendoodles tend to have more predictable temperaments. F1s are generally balanced, while Multigens tend to have a more Poodle-like temperament. F2s are the least predictable, with personality traits that can vary widely.

Energy Levels

Energy levels can range from moderate in F1s and F2s to higher in Multigen Goldendoodles, particularly if they have a strong Poodle influence. Families with young children or busy lifestyles should consider how much exercise and attention the dog will need.

Training and Intelligence

All generations of Goldendoodles are intelligent and trainable, but Multigens may require more mental stimulation due to their higher Poodle content. F1s and F2s are generally easier to train as family pets because of their Golden Retriever influence, which makes them eager to please.

Common Questions About Personality and Home Suitability:

Which Goldendoodle generation is best for apartment living?

F1 Goldendoodles are generally adaptable to apartment living due to their balanced energy levels. However, as long as they receive enough exercise and mental stimulation, even Multigen Goldendoodles can thrive in smaller spaces.

Are Multigen Goldendoodles more independent than F1s?

Yes, because they have more Poodle genetics, Multigen Goldendoodles may be more independent and reserved compared to F1

Goldendoodles, which are known for their sociable and easygoing nature.

Which Goldendoodle generation is best for families with young children?

F1 Goldendoodles are often recommended for families with young children due to their balanced and predictable temperament, making them friendly and patient companions. F2 and Multigen Goldendoodles can also be good with children, but their energy levels and personality traits may vary.

Do F2 Goldendoodles require more attention than F1s?

It depends on the individual dog. Some F2s may have higher energy levels or more demanding temperaments, requiring more attention and exercise, while others may be calmer and more laid-back. Early socialization and training will help shape their behavior.

In summary, F1 Goldendoodles tend to be more balanced and versatile, making them ideal for a wide range of families and living situations. F2s are more variable in temperament, while Multigen Goldendoodles are often higher in energy and more consistent in personality but may require more stimulation and training.

More independent traits and over-attachment (often called "Velcro dog syndrome") can both manifest in Goldendoodles, depending on the specific mix of genetics they inherit from their Poodle and Golden Retriever ancestors, as well as individual personality and environment. Here's how these traits can present and which generations or types of Goldendoodles might be more prone to them:

Independent Traits in Goldendoodles

More independent traits typically arise from the Poodle side of the Goldendoodle's heritage. Poodles, especially Standard Poodles, tend to be intelligent, alert, and sometimes more aloof compared to the very sociable and people-oriented Golden Retriever. If a Goldendoodle inherits more Poodle-like traits, independence can manifest in several ways:

Less Constant Need for Attention

Independent Goldendoodles may not follow their owners around as much or constantly seek attention. They can be content spending time alone, making them potentially better suited for households where people are not always home.

More Reserved with Strangers

These dogs may be more aloof or cautious around new people or visitors, taking time to warm up compared to more social and friendly types. While they're still affectionate with their family, they may not be as immediately outgoing with strangers.

Self-Entertaining

Independent Goldendoodles may be more capable of entertaining themselves, engaging with toys or exploring on their own without requiring constant interaction. This can be beneficial in busy households where the dog can't always have direct attention.

Less "Velcro" Behavior

While still affectionate, they may not exhibit the clinginess associated with Golden Retriever-heavy Goldendoodles. They're happy to be around their people but don't feel the need to always be by their side.

Over-Attachment (Velcro Dog Syndrome) in Goldendoodles

On the other hand, over-attachment, often referred to as "Velcro dog syndrome," is more closely associated with the Golden Retriever traits. Goldendoodles that inherit more Golden Retriever personality traits tend to be extremely people-oriented and can develop strong bonds with their family members. Over-attachment can manifest in the following ways:

- Overly attached Goldendoodles will follow their owners around the house, rarely leaving their side. They may even have difficulty staying alone, always wanting to be in the same room as their humans.
- Over-attachment can also lead to separation anxiety and Goldendoodles with strong Golden Retriever traits may become anxious or distressed when left alone for extended periods. They may exhibit behaviors like barking, destructive chewing, or attempts to escape when left by themselves. Velcro-type Goldendoodles (from their Golden Retriever heritage) may struggle with being alone for long stretches of time, making them better suited for families where someone is often home or they can be provided with company throughout the day.

Which Generations/Types Are More Prone to These Traits?

Independent Traits

Goldendoodles with more Poodle genetics (such as F2B, F3, and F4 Multigen Goldendoodles) are more likely to exhibit independent traits. Poodles are known for their intelligence and reserved nature, so as the percentage of Poodle influence increases through selective breeding, these dogs may be more comfortable spending time on their own and require less attention compared to earlier generations.

Over-Attachment (Velcro Dogs)

F1 and F1B Goldendoodles are more likely to develop over-attachment due to their Golden Retriever influence. Golden Retrievers are famously loyal, affectionate, and people-focused, which can lead to strong bonds and sometimes clingy behavior. F1s are a direct 50/50 mix of Golden Retriever and Poodle, so this trait is more common in them. In F1Bs, where the mix may lean more toward Golden Retriever, the potential for Velcro-like behavior can be even more pronounced.

F1B Goldendoodles, while still affectionate, may show a slightly lower tendency for clinginess compared to F1s due to the higher Poodle influence. Poodles can be more independent, so F1Bs may not always exhibit the same level of attachment. However, individual dogs can still display strong Velcro tendencies, especially if they inherit more of the Golden Retriever's personality traits.

Multigen Goldendoodles, especially those with a higher percentage of Poodle genetics, may be less Velcro-like than F1s or F1Bs. With more Poodle influence, these dogs tend to be slightly more independent, although they can still be affectionate and loyal. They may not exhibit the same level of clinginess but still enjoy close companionship.

Typical Goldendoodle Sizes by Type

Goldendoodles generally come in three size categories: **Standard**, **Miniature**, and **Toy**. The size of a Goldendoodle is primarily determined by the size of the Poodle parent.

1. Standard Goldendoodles

• **Weight:** 50 to 90 pounds

• **Height:** 20 to 26 inches at the shoulder

• **Common Generations:** F1, F1B, F2, Multigen

• **Description:** Standard Goldendoodles are the largest variety, resulting from a Standard Poodle and a Golden Retriever. F1 and F1B Standard Goldendoodles are typically on the larger side, especially if both parent breeds are large. F2 and Multigen Standard Goldendoodles may vary slightly in size but generally fall within this range.

2. Miniature Goldendoodles

- **Weight:** 25 to 45 pounds
- **Height:** 15 to 20 inches at the shoulder
- **Common Generations:** F1B, F2B, Multigen

Description: Miniature Goldendoodles are a cross between a Miniature Poodle and a Golden Retriever or another Goldendoodle. These dogs are a medium size, suitable for smaller homes or those who want a more manageable size than a Standard.

3. Toy (or Petite) Goldendoodles

- **Weight:** 10 to 25 pounds
- **Height:** 10 to 15 inches at the shoulder
- **Common Generations:** F1B, F2B, Multigen

Description: Toy or Petite Goldendoodles are the smallest variety, often a result of breeding a Toy Poodle with a smaller Golden Retriever or another smaller Goldendoodle. These dogs are ideal for those living in apartments or smaller spaces.

Size Predictors for Goldendoodles

Poodle Parent's Size

The size of the Poodle parent is one of the strongest predictors of how large a Goldendoodle will grow. If the Poodle parent is a Standard, Miniature, or Toy, this will directly influence whether the Goldendoodle will fall into the Standard, Miniature, or Toy size range. For example, if a Standard Poodle is used, you can expect the dog to be larger, whereas a Miniature or Toy Poodle will likely produce a smaller Goldendoodle.

Generation

The generation of the Goldendoodle can impact size, though this tends to be more subtle:

F1 (50% Golden Retriever, 50% Poodle): F1 Goldendoodles, especially those with Standard Poodles, are more likely to be on the larger side, often growing to Standard size.

F1B (75% Poodle, 25% Golden Retriever): F1Bs with Miniature or Toy Poodles tend to be smaller due to the higher percentage of Poodle genetics.

Multigen: The size of Multigen Goldendoodles is more predictable if breeders have carefully selected for a specific size, particularly in Miniature or Toy varieties.

Parents' Sizes

Looking at the size of both the Golden Retriever and the Poodle parent can give you a good idea of the potential adult size of a Goldendoodle. The weight and height of the parents are a reliable indicator, especially if the breeding line has been consistent.

While not a foolproof method, many breeders and dog owners look at a puppy's paw size as an indicator of their eventual adult size. Larger paws often suggest a larger adult dog, especially when comparing puppies within the same litter.

Growth Curve by Age

Goldendoodles tend to reach about half of their adult weight by 4 to 5 months of age. You can usually estimate their full adult size by doubling their weight at this point. This isn't an exact science, but it's a helpful rule of thumb for many owners. Additionally, knowing the size of the Poodle parent (Standard, Miniature, or

Toy) can help predict whether your dog will be a Standard, Miniature, or Toy Goldendoodle.

Standard Goldendoodles: Usually finish growing between 12 to 16 months of age and are usually 50-90 pounds.

Miniature and Toy Goldendoodles: Often reach their adult size by 10 to 12 months. Miniature Goldendoodles are 25-45 pounds, and Toy/Petite Goldendoodles are 10-25 pounds. Remember, the parents' sizes are the best predictor.

There can also be size variability within the same litter, especially in F1 or F2 generations, as some puppies may inherit more Golden Retriever traits (making them larger) or more Poodle traits (making them smaller).

It means that if size is an important factor for you, consider getting an F1B, F2B, or Multigen Goldendoodle from a reputable breeder who has experience breeding for a specific size, such as Miniature or Toy. These later generations are often more predictable in terms of size.

Food and Feeding

As we discuss later, you need to get your puppy into a regular schedule. The quicker you can do this and get him used to this schedule, the easier everything becomes. Creating a schedule really can make a big difference.

Feeding them to the same schedule also means that they will want to relieve themselves in reaction to that schedule. This, in itself, will make it easier for you to house-train.

Before we talk about the training it's good to know the basics of how much and what to feed your pup. Here we also include what to avoid and the common problem of 'gulping'.

What to Feed

Dogs are built to be meat-eaters, but they are descended from omnivores, so they can survive adequately without meat (if the protein balance is right).

The protein in meat is not the same as the protein found in plant-based foods, and this is one of the reasons to be careful of the food you give your puppy and your dog.

This doesn't mean that dogs can't live on a plant-based diet; it just means it will need to be supplemented with the essential proteins that he will require as well as Vitamin D.

Balancing nutrition is the most important aspect of your dogs' food. For example, we need our carbs for energy, but dogs don't need many carbs.

Dogs, and especially puppies, need fats and fatty acids. Most of these are contained in animal fats, but some seed and plant oils can provide a concentrated source of energy. You are looking for an Omega-3 family of essential fatty acids.

When looking for dog food, look at the type of calories rather than the overall total. For example, you don't want too much carbo-hydrate.

Today's average dog food can contain anywhere between 30% and 70% carbohydrates, but in the wild, dogs will intake only about 15%.

An adult dog's diet can contain up to 50% carbohydrate (by weight), up to 4.5% fibre, and a minimum of around 5.5% should come from fats, and 10% from protein.

You can read more about nutrition at nap.edu, and this is listed in the resources at the end of this book.

In general, though, if you want to check out how much meat is in your dog food, look at the ingredients list. The further down the meat appears, the lower the meat content.

The most common ingredients today are whole grain, fat, soya, and corn. So if you see chicken by-products, this doesn't mean it is chicken meat. It most likely isn't.

The top ingredients to look for (and look for a range of these in the same food) include deboned chicken or turkey, Atlantic mackerel and herring, chicken and turkey liver, chicken and turkey heart, and other items such as egg and other types of fish. All high in protein.

There has also been some debate about dry food versus wet food. The main difference being that wet food contains more water (around 75%) whereas dry food can contain only about 10% water.

Dry food tends to be more calorie-dense, and wet food has less grain and fewer carbs. Grain isn't necessarily a bad thing, it just depends on quantity.

Dry food lasts for longer and tend to be more cost-effective than wet food.

There are lots of choices on the market, and you will want to research this for yourself.

It's important to vary their food and its texture from time-to-time to give them a little change. Like many smaller dogs, Poodles can be fussy eaters so varying their diet (and sometimes portion size) can keep them engaged and interested in their food. You may also discover something that they love and decide to stick with it.

Some owners also like to feed their dog a raw diet known as RAW or a BARF diet (Bones and Raw Food). There are quite a few sites online that can explain how to do this and what this diet includes. A key to this diet is balance and The Natural Dog site (A Guide to

Raw Diet and Health The Natural Way) is a good place to start if this is something that you are interested in finding more about.

How Much to Feed

Puppies can require up to double the energy intake of adult dogs. This is based on the weight of your puppy - it doesn't mean they eat twice as much as an adult dog, just that per pound of weight they do.

Depending on your type of Poodle, they will reach their adult weight anywhere between 5 and 14 months old. You can check the table in Chapter 2 for the expected size and weight.

Although Poodles can be fussy eaters they also love to eat - probably as a result of their constant energy. It can mean that it is best to control their feeding and not leave food in their bowl for them to nibble on between meals.

The frequency really does depend on how old they are. A puppy's tummy is small and it grows over time. This means that you need to feed smaller amounts more regularly, the younger they are.

Puppies aged 8-16 weeks need to be fed 4 meals a day, perhaps every 3 hours. Pups ages 3 to 6 months should be fed 3 times a day (every 4 hours) and then after that twice a day, in the morning and early evening.

Your aim is to spread their nutrition throughout the day, so space out the times to equal intervals across the day. Once you are taking your puppy out for walks, which will mean more exercise, remember not to feed your puppy just before or after exercise.

The amount that you feed your puppy will depend on their weight and age. The dog food you choose will also have a variety of different protein levels.

When you decide on your dog food, the packaging will tell you how much to feed your puppy (depending on their weight). If you are in any doubt, ask your veterinarian.

Gulping

Gulping is term that is used in this context for eating too fast. It's not uncommon for dogs to eat quickly, and many dogs, especially puppies, tend to gulp down their food out of excitement or habit.

However, chronic fast eating can lead to potential health issues, so it's important to monitor your dog and take steps to slow down their eating if necessary. Here's a more detailed look at whether you should be concerned and how to address it:

Is Eating Fast a Problem?

While fast eating is common, especially in dogs with high energy levels like Goldendoodles, it can lead to several problems if not managed:

Choking
When a dog eats too quickly, they may not chew their food properly, increasing the risk of choking on large pieces of kibble or food.

Digestive Issues
Gulping food can cause your dog to swallow air along with their food, which may lead to gas, bloating, or vomiting after meals. Fast eaters are also more likely to experience indigestion or discomfort because their stomach is overwhelmed by the rapid intake.

Bloat (Gastric Dilatation-Volvulus or GDV)

One of the most serious concerns for fast eaters, particularly larger, deep-chested breeds like Standard Goldendoodles, is bloat. When a dog eats too quickly and swallows air, their stomach can expand and twist, cutting off blood flow to vital organs. This condition is life-threatening and requires immediate veterinary attention.

Weight Gain

Fast eaters may not recognize when they're full, leading to overeating and, in some cases, obesity. This can happen if they finish their meals so quickly that they don't feel satisfied and beg for more food.

Why Do Some Dogs Eat So Fast?

There are several reasons why dogs may eat quickly:

Instinct

In the wild, dogs had to eat quickly to avoid competition with other pack members or predators. While your dog is safe at home, this instinct may still be present, especially in puppies or rescue dogs who may have experienced food insecurity in the past.

Excitement

Many dogs get very excited at mealtime, leading them to gulp their food without realising it. This excitement can build up if the dog has learned to associate mealtime with something highly rewarding.

Hunger

If your dog has gone too long between meals, they may be extra hungry and more likely to eat quickly. Ensuring they are fed at regular intervals can help mitigate this behaviour.

Competition

In multi-dog households, dogs may eat fast out of a sense of competition, even if the other dog isn't trying to take their food. This behaviour can become habitual over time.

How to Slow Down a Fast Eater

If your dog is eating too quickly, here are some strategies to help slow them down and promote healthier eating habits:

Slow Feeder Bowls

These bowls are designed with ridges or mazes that make it more difficult for your dog to gulp down large mouthfuls of food. By forcing your dog to eat around obstacles, they naturally slow their eating pace.

Smaller, More Frequent Meals

Feed your dog smaller portions throughout the day. This helps prevent them from consuming too much food at once and reduces the urgency they may feel to eat quickly.

Puzzle Feeders or Food Toys

Puzzle feeders or treat-dispensing toys can turn mealtime into a mentally stimulating activity, requiring your dog to work for their food. This slows down eating and provides enrichment.

Spread the Food Out

Instead of placing all the food in a bowl, spread it out on a flat surface, like a baking sheet or a large mat. This forces your dog to pick up smaller bites, slowing the pace.

Hand-Feeding

Hand-feeding can help you control the pace of your dog's eating and encourage them to chew each bite more thoroughly.

Add Water to Dry Food:

Adding a little water to your dog's kibble can slow down their eating, as they have to lap up the liquid along with the food. It can also help with digestion.

When to Talk to a Veterinarian

If your dog has always eaten quickly and isn't experiencing any digestive issues, you may not need to worry too much. However, you should be concerned if your dog:

- Vomits or regurgitates food regularly after eating.
- Exhibits signs of bloat (restlessness, pacing, swollen abdomen, retching without vomiting).
- Is gagging, choking, or struggling to breathe during or after meals.
- Gains weight rapidly or seems constantly hungry despite regular meals.

In these cases, consult your veterinarian. They can rule out any underlying health issues and help you find strategies to address your dog's fast eating habits.

Dangerous Foods

Feeding your Goldendoodle a well-balanced diet is important, but it's just as crucial to be aware of foods that are toxic or harmful to them. Some common human foods can cause anything from mild digestive issues to severe, life-threatening conditions in dogs. Here's a list of the most common human foods that we might not think about, including how much is considered dangerous:

1. Alcohol

Why it's dangerous: Alcohol can cause ethanol poisoning, leading to slowed breathing, decreased heart rate, vomiting, tremors, coma, or death.

How much is dangerous: Even small amounts (a few licks) can cause poisoning in dogs. Never give alcohol to your dog, and keep beverages like beer, wine, and spirits well out of reach.

2. Chocolate and Cocoa

Why it's dangerous: Chocolate contains theobromine and caffeine, which are toxic to dogs. Theobromine affects the heart, kidneys, lungs, and nervous system.

How much is dangerous: The darker the chocolate, the more dangerous it is. For example:

- Milk chocolate: 1 ounce per pound of body weight can be toxic.
- Dark chocolate: As little as 0.1 ounces per pound of body weight can cause symptoms.

- Baking chocolate: Even smaller amounts (0.1 ounce for a 20-pound dog) can be fatal.

A medium size dog can be affected by just 6 small squares of baking chocolate, but it would take nearly ¾ lb. of milk chocolate to have the same affect. If your puppy or dog has eaten dark chocolate contact your vet immediately. You will be asked the weight of your dog so its useful to always check his weight regularly. Symptoms include seizures, vomiting, diarrhoea, excitement, tremors, abnormal heart rate/rhythm, staggering, and even coma.

3. Caffeine

Why it's dangerous: Caffeine, found in coffee, tea, energy drinks, and some chocolates, affects the central nervous system and heart, leading to restlessness, rapid heart rate, vomiting, and potentially death.

How much is dangerous: Ingesting even a small amount, such as from coffee grounds or tea bags, can cause symptoms. Dogs can be seriously affected by 150 mg of caffeine per kilogram of body weight (equivalent to around 2 teaspoons of instant coffee for a 10-pound dog).

4. Grapes and Raisins

Why they're dangerous: Grapes and raisins can cause kidney failure in dogs, though the exact toxin is still unknown.

This also includes other dried variants like sultanas and currants and any foods containing grape, such as grape juice, raisin cereal, raisin bread, granola, trail mix, and raisin cookies or bars. Early signs are vomiting, diarrhoea, and lethargy. One of the most common causes is from your dog eating wild bird food. Ground feeders should be enclosed which only allow birds to enter.

How much is dangerous: Even small amounts can be toxic, with as little as a few grapes or raisins potentially causing kidney damage in dogs. If your dog ingests any amount, seek veterinary care immediately.

5. Onions, Garlic, and Chives

Why they're dangerous: These foods contain thiosulfate, which can cause the destruction of red blood cells, leading to anemia and dogs don't have the liver enzyme necessary to digest it. The amount required will depend on body weight. It is toxic in raw, cooked or dried form

How much is dangerous: Eating just 0.5% of your dog's body weight in onions or garlic can cause toxicity. For example, around 50 grams (1.75 ounces) of onion can be toxic to a 10-pound dog.

6. Macadamia Nuts

Why they're dangerous: Macadamia nuts can cause weakness, vomiting, hyperthermia (fever), and tremors.

How much is dangerous: Toxicity has been reported with as little as 2.4 grams per kilogram of body weight. Even a few nuts can cause symptoms in small dogs.

7. Xylitol (Artificial Sweetener)

Why it's dangerous: Xylitol causes a rapid release of insulin, leading to hypoglycemia (low blood sugar), seizures, liver failure, and even death.

Xylitol is used as a sweetener in several products including candy, gum, baked goods, diet foods, and even some peanut butter and toothpaste.

How much is dangerous: As little as 0.1 grams per kilogram of body weight can cause hypoglycemia. For a small dog, this can mean a single piece of sugar-free gum.

8. Avocado (Persin)

Why it's dangerous: Avocados contain persin, which can cause vomiting, diarrhea, and heart congestion in dogs.

How much is dangerous: While the flesh of the avocado is less toxic, the pit, leaves, and bark contain high amounts of persin. Ingesting any part of the avocado plant can lead to toxicity.

9. Raw Potato and Unripe Tomatoes

Why they're dangerous: Potatoes and tomatoes contain solanine, a toxin that can cause gastrointestinal issues, lethargy, and neurological symptoms. Solanin (and tomatin) in particularly found in the green parts of the tomato plant (leaves, stems, of unripe tomatoes). Ripe tomatoes are generally considered safe for dogs in small amounts .

Raw Potato's also contain solanine which is mainly found in green or sprouted potatoes. Cooking potatoes reduces the solanine content, making them safe for dogs to eat in moderation when fully cooked.

It can cause serious symptoms like vomiting, diarrhea, lethargy, and confusion in high doses.

How much is dangerous: While small amounts may not be fatal, ingestion of large quantities can be toxic, especially if the potatoes are raw or the tomatoes unripe.

10. Bones

Why they're dangerous: Cooked bones, in particular, can splinter and cause choking, internal blockages, or punctures in the digestive tract.

How much is dangerous: Any cooked bone is a hazard. Raw bones can be safer but should always be given under supervision to avoid choking.

11. Nuts (Pecans, Almonds, Walnuts) and Cherry, peach, apricot and plum stones

The pits (stones) of **cherries, peaches, apricots, and plums** naturally contain amygdalin, which can release cyanide when chewed or broken. Cyanide poisoning in dogs can cause symptoms such as vomiting, labored breathing, dilated pupils, rapid heart rate (tachycardia), cardiac arrhythmias, and eventually coma. Urgent veterinary treatment is essential if cyanide poisoning is suspected, as it can be life-threatening.

In addition the leaves, fruit, seeds and bark of avocados contain Persin, which will cause vomiting and diarrhoea. (**Pecans, Almonds, Walnuts, Macadamia**) - these have the potential to not only cause vomiting but possible pancreatitis. Walnuts, especially moldy ones, can cause tremors and seizures.

How much is dangerous: Even a small handful of nuts can cause gastrointestinal distress or more serious symptoms in dogs.

12. Coconut

Coconut flesh and coconut oil are not toxic to dogs but may cause stomach upset or diarrhea if consumed in large quantities. Coconut water, however, should not be given to dogs because it contains high levels of potassium, which can lead to hyperkalemia and potential heart issues.

13. Shellfish

Some dogs may be sensitive or allergic to shellfish (such as prawns or langoustine), causing vomiting, diarrhea, or other reactions even with small amounts and one of my own dogs has a severe reaction to prawns. While shellfish can cause issues for some dogs, fish is generally safe and even beneficial when cooked properly. Fish is a good source of protein and omega-3 fatty acids, but it should always be cooked thoroughly and cooled to avoid parasites and bacteria, and any bones should be removed.

What to do if your pet is poisoned

These are the instructions from the Pet Poison helpline:-

1. **Remove your pet from the area** where the potential poisoning occurred to prevent further exposure.
2. **Check your pet's condition** to ensure they are safe, breathing normally, and not showing signs of immediate distress.

3. **Do NOT give any home antidotes** (such as hydrogen peroxide) without professional advice.
4. **Do NOT induce vomiting** unless instructed to do so by a veterinarian or the Pet Poison Helpline. Inducing vomiting can sometimes make the situation worse, depending on the substance ingested.
5. **Contact your veterinarian or the Pet Poison Helpline immediately** for guidance. In the U.S., you can call the Pet Poison Helpline.
6. **If veterinary attention is necessary,** go to your nearest veterinarian or emergency clinic immediately.

Important Tip

It's always better to act quickly when dealing with a potential poisoning. **Do not wait** for your dog to show symptoms before seeking help. There is often a narrow window of time in which decontamination (such as inducing vomiting or stomach pumping) can be performed, so report the situation immediately.

Generally speaking, if your puppy is being sick, then you can expect the following advice:-

If your puppy is vomiting, although it can be a sign of obstruction, it can be caused things such as gastritis, intestinal parasites, ingestion of a foreign body, infections, and so on.

In any case of vomiting, the first thing to do is give the stomach time to rest which means no food for 8-12 hours.

Don't give things like Pepto Bismol or Imodium. You can start on a Pepcid AC (famotidine) tablet every 12 hours for 2-3 days. This can be bought over the counter in most pharmacies. Check with your vet on the dosage as this will be governed by weight and age.

After 8-12 hours offer a small amount of water. Wait half hour, if no vomiting, offer a small amount of rice (50%) and boiled boneless chicken 4-6 times a day. Keep him on this diet a few days before slowly returning to his regular food.

If he continues to vomit after doing this then he needs to be seen by a veterinarian.

This exchange, in a vet forum for Goldendoodles when the puppy was being sick might be the prefect example of what some of you might come across when your puppy is around 6-7 months old.

"Admin: I'll do all I can to help. Hopefully it didn't make a mess. Did the Golden eat anything unusual?

"Customer: let's see, part of my couch, and some toys within the past few weeks, we are watching her like hawks and have had to throw away her toys."

From couches, to chair legs, to sock, shoes (just the ones you love most), bank cards, spectacles the list goes on. Puppies chew things. And always the things we really don't want them to. The best way to manage this is to think about the things you love, or use, the most and then place them well out of reach.

Bear this in mind as we now mover on to training your puppy over the rest of this boo.

(In the case of the above example, although the vetinerarian was enquiring about food, eating things can cause a blockage, so if you are at all worried take you puppy to the vet).

Planning Ahead

Before you bring your puppy to his forever home, you need to find out what type of food your puppy has been eating up until this point. Your breeder will be happy to let you know and should provide you with a starter pack of what they have been feeding his. Don't worry if they don't do this as standard practice, just make sure that you know what you need to have in the house for the arrival of your new puppy.

You will introduce him to the food you want to use slowly by mixing some of his existing food into the new food that you have chosen. Slowly increase the proportion of his new food over a period of 7-10 days. You also need to know how often he was being fed, and at what time because, initially, you will stick to this pattern and gradually change it if you need to do so.

You do this because any sudden change to his diet will upset his tummy. It will make him feel uncomfortable and can result in unexpected accidents caused by diarrhoea which your puppy won't be able to control. It simply makes it more difficult to successfully start potty training in these first few important days.

As you start to slowly change over his food you can also start to gradually change the time at which he gets his food so that the schedule moves to the times that works within your household.

If you need to change his food at any point in his life then you will always repeat the process of gradually mixing in the old food with the new. Dogs - and their stomachs - don't like a sudden change to their diet so always remember to introduce a new dog food slowly, no matter how old he is.

In order to get help him settle quickly in his new home you will need to make sure that you have something that smells familiar to him when he arrives. If the breeder doesn't have something you can take home with you, then ask if you can leave some clothing for him for a at least a week so that you can take it home with your puppy (a sock or an old towel will do).

Once he arrives home, put this item into the crate or basket that you want his to use. This will give your puppy some comfort over the first few days, and be a familiar smell which should help him settle in.

Finally, if you have a yard or garden, you will need to puppy-proof it. If there are any gaps in a fence or hedge, your puppy will find it, and he will disappear in a second to go exploring. You can use plastic chicken-wire or something similar but anything that will securely block access will do.

Don't forget that your puppy will want to chew things inside the home too, so you will need to puppy-proof any electrical wires (move them out of reach if you can) along with house-plants, some of which are poisonous to him.

You will want all of the family involved in his early training and you need to think about this before he arrives. Work out who can do what and try and get all your household members on board as early as you can (this is also good for helping to prevent separation anxiety). You might want to try and get agreement on who does the morning, or lunch or evening care or who's job it is to think up a game to play on a particular day.

And don't forget to pick the name of your puppy!

How to choose a name

Your puppy might already have a name, but if you are reading this before you have picked your puppy's name, then here are a few tips which can help you decide. A good name can even make training easier.

Dogs hear at a higher frequency range than we do, and so choosing a name that ends with a vowel sound will help to grab his attention.

Names that end in an 'ie ar 'ay' sound are best. Ideally, the name should start with a hard letter sound like B or D, and ideally, it should contain two syllables. For example Millie, Poppy, Barney, Paddy or even Tootsie.

But remember, you want to avoid any names that your puppy might confuse with one of your cues (like sit, stay, down, here or come).

Try and say the name a few times too because you need to make sure all the members of your family can say it - especially if they are toddlers - and that everyone is comfortable to shout the name in the park.

Although it's better to use his name from the very start, don't worry if you take a day or two to find just the right name that seems to fit your puppy's personality as you get to know him over these first few days.

If you have a dog from a shelter, and you really want to change his name, or don't know what his name used to be, then give him a few days to get used to it (but it might take him a bit longer).

To him get to know his name you need to help him along. When you say it, reward him at the same time even if there is no response. Then, as soon as there is a response, for example he looks in your direction, immediately reward him with a tastier treat and lots of praise. In the beginning he will be responding to the sound of your voice rather than to his name but he will soon put two and two together.

Walk around the house and say his name and reward his response. Getting your puppy used to his name can be fun for all of us.

Welcome home

When your pup comes home, you will ideally already have his crate or basket ready. You will have the same type of dog food that he was being fed, and you will have the item placed in his crate or basket that smells familiar to his from his previous home.

Over the first few nights, he is likely to miss his old family. It is okay, over the first nights, to take his crate or basket into your room, but only do this for the first few nights.

He also won't be used to lots of noise and activity around him. Try and keep things as calm as possible, and make sure to remember to allow him some 'time-outs'.

To introduce him to his crate, place it in the room that you tend to spend most of your time. If you have a room you want your puppy to stay in, then, after a day or two, move the crate into this room - but make sure you and the rest of the family spend time with him in that room. We will cover crate training in chapter 9.

And don't forget that puppies sleep a lot and they need their sleep. They will easily sleep for 7-8 hours at night, and they can sleep up to 14 hours a day. I will talk about a schedule later.

But, in the early days, try to make sure that he gets his sleep time. Everyone will want to play with him. This is okay, and it's good for your puppy to have lots of affection and attention because it will help him to get familiar with people and being handled, but try and ensure that he gets a little break to get some sleep.

In terms of picking him up and cuddling him, try not to overdo his handling. Constantly picking him up will be something his little body is unlikely to be used to. Just like us, if we get picked up too much, it can become uncomfortable and even painful.

This isn't anything to worry about, but it's useful to be aware of how often he is being handled.

The best way to pick up your young puppy is to put your hands around his chest, then pull him towards your chest. As soon as he is safely secured, take one of your hands and use it to support his bottom so that you are supporting his weight - much like a baby.

Finally, don't forget to take a sniff of his breath. A puppy's breath has a unique smell, so grab your chance while you can. It disappears quickly!

Vaccinations over the first year

It's a good idea to talk to your vet about your puppy's vaccination requirements as soon as you can. Below is a summary of the recommended vaccinations from the American Kennel Club. There are some other vaccinations so talk to your local veterinary about any requirements in your area.

Recommended vaccinations:

- 6-8 weeks - Distemper, parvovirus
- 10-12 weeks - DHPP (for distemper, adenovirus (hepatitis), parainfluenza, parvovirus
- 16-18 weeks DHPP, rabies
- 12-16 months DHPP, rabies

Unvaccinated puppies less than 4 months old are most at risk of Parvovirus. This is contagious and affects all dogs and there is no cure and is one of the main reason that you don't want your unvaccinated puppy to meet any dogs that you don't know.

You can take him to your yard around 7 days after his first set of vaccinations, but still avoid other dogs especially if you don't know them. Your yard must be enclosed to ensure no other dogs have been there. Don't let his feet touch the ground in public spaces.

If you live in an apartment, you might need to go outside to a public or well-used street during his potty training so that he can relieve himself. Pick one spot, and carry him there and back but you can let him sniff around that spot.

After his second vaccination, you can take him for a walk on paved surfaces, but not on grass or places where you can't see if other dogs have urinated or gone to the toilet.

It is still important for his not to meet unfamiliar dogs.

The Kennel Club recommends talking to your veterinarian about heartworm treatment when your puppy is 12-16 weeks old. This is a preventative medication that is taken regularly.

These are the sort of issues where any recommendation must come from a qualified pet health professional who understands the laws, and problems in your area, and who will be aware of any breed-specific problems. Make sure that you ask your veterinarian for advice.

Your puppy can go outside for a walk in the park after his third set of vaccinations (around weeks 16-18). It is also at this point that he can exercise for up to 20 minutes at a time.

Finally, he can meet unfamiliar dogs. At this stage, when he is around 18 weeks, you can also take him to his puppy socialization classes at the local pet store or your vet (and where all the puppies will be at the same vaccination stage).

Socialization

In its simplest form, socialization is how you and your puppy learn to communicate with each other and how your puppy learns about those that he lives with or meets. It is how he learns to live in 'society' and how to interact with thing he meets including humans and other dogs.

Having as many happy encounters as possible during his early weeks helps his to relate appropriately to humans of all ages, other dogs and to situations that he will face day-to-day throughout his life.

This isn't easy in the first week or two because your puppy has yet to be vaccinated.

However, you can still carry him, take him out in your car, and have friends and family come to the house to meet him. Try and let him meet as many adults and children as you can in the weeks before you can take him to classes. He should also meet other dogs at home if you know them, and you know that they are fully vaccinated.

This is also the best time to touch his ears, mouth, tails, and paws and to get his used to you doing this. This part of puppy training is often missed, but it will really help later with grooming, or if you need to inspect him for an injury or when he goes to the vet for an examination.

Sit with him quietly so that you are also teaching him how to relax with you, and touch his ears or mouth, run your hand over his paws and his tail, and give him a treat and reward when he remains calm and relaxed.

If you can, and as soon as you are allowed - and after his vaccinations allow it - take your puppy to socialization classes so that he can meet other young puppies and their parents.

They will play around for 20 or 30 minutes, but they learn how to communicate with dogs that they don't know and they will learn how 'far they can go'. Dogs are pretty good at letting each other know when enough-is-enough! They also learn about meeting new humans who are not part of the family.

This part of his early training helps him feel comfortable with dogs he doesn't know and he will learn what he can and can't do without getting a bark or, occasionally a nip, and he will be learning about meeting and interacting with humans.

House and Potty Training

One of the main reasons people hesitate to get a puppy is the thought of potty training, or more specifically, the fear of having a dog that isn't house-trained and makes a mess in the home. Potty training your puppy will be one of the first things you tackle when they come home, and while it may seem daunting, don't worry—it can be done! In fact, in a few years, you'll probably forget you even had to house-train your beloved dog and won't remember how you did it.

Every puppy learns at their own pace, and the speed at which they become house-trained can vary. Some puppies may already have had a head start if their previous home or breeder began basic training, even at a young age.

How Long Can a Puppy Hold On?

A puppy's bladder is small and grows with them, so they will need to relieve themselves more frequently when they are young. As a general rule, puppies can hold their bladder for about one hour per month of age. For example, a one-month-old puppy can hold it for about an hour, and a two-month-old should manage around two hours. It's important not to push them to hold it for longer than this, as accidents will happen if they have to wait beyond this time when they are young.

Typically, puppies under six months (and young dogs) won't be able to hold their bladder for more than three or four hours. This means you'll need to plan around this timing f you're going to be out much longer than this. Either pop back at lunchtime, or have someone drop in to let them out.

A puppy under 6 months old will typically poop around 3 to 5 times a day, depending on factors like diet, feeding schedule, activity level, and overall health. Puppies have smaller digestive systems, so they process food more quickly, leading to more frequent bowel movements and a regular feeding schedules can help create a more predictable potty routine. As they grow older, their digestive system matures, and the frequency will likely decrease.

Puppies often need to poop shortly after eating, usually within 5 to 30 minutes. If you're about to leave the house, feed your puppy around 45 minutes beforehand and then take them out for a bathroom break before you go. Playing with your puppy can also stimulate them to poop, so take them out after playtime as well.

Puppy Pads

While puppy pads can be useful, they shouldn't replace frequent outdoor potty trips. The best thing I've found for potty training is puppy pads that resemble grass—they work incredibly well.

When using pads, start by placing them in the room where your puppy will spend most of their time. As soon as you notice your puppy showing signs that they need to go (circling, sniffing, or being restless), place them on the pad. If they use it, reward them with plenty of praise. You don't need to use puppy pads, you could, instead, take them to their outside spot as soon as you see these signs but this will be harder if it takes longer to get there.

Once your puppy regularly uses the pad, gradually move it closer to the door they'll use when going outside. Take your time with this process, only moving the pad a small distance each day. Eventually, place the pad outside the door, and your puppy will start associating going outside with potty time. If accidents happen, don't panic—place an emergency pad nearby and take your puppy outside as soon as possible. Always give lots of praise for every small success.

Managing Potty Training

During potty training, your puppy will need plenty of praise and positive reinforcement. Every time they go outside to relieve themselves, praise him and give him a treat—but wait he's completely finished - puppies tend to get distracted if you reward them mid-potty!

You can also use a specific phrase, like "potty" or "pee-pee," to help them associate the action with the word. Consistency is key, and this phrase will be useful as your dog gets older.

One important tip: never punish your puppy for accidents. Don't get angry or push their nose in the mess; they won't understand and could become anxious about pottying in front of you. Positive reinforcement will go much further in helping them learn.

Leaving the House and Overnight

Your puppy may not be able to hold their bladder through the night until they are several months old, so be prepared for night-time bathroom trips. To minimise this, start the bedtime routine of taking them outside to potty before they go to bed, and first things in the morning when they wake up.

If their crate is big enough place puppy pads in the corner of their crate (but they don't tend to potty in their crate) and near where they sleep, but be sure to take them outside first thing in the morning.

Your puppy will eventually start settling into a bedtime routine, but at first, when they wake up during the night needing to go, avoid turning on bright lights or playing with them—take them outside calmly and return them straight to bed afterward.

During potty training, you may want to remove their water bowl a couple of hours before bedtime, but always make sure they have access to water during the day. This helps reduce the need for nighttime bathroom breaks.

Clean Up

Cleaning up after accidents is part of the process, but using the right products is important. Avoid ammonia-based cleaners, as these can encourage your puppy to go in the same spot again. Cold water works well for removing stains, or you can use a mixture of biological powder or vinegar and water.

Setting a Schedule

Establishing a consistent schedule is one of the most effective ways to potty train your puppy. Take them out as soon as they wake up, after meals, after drinking, and after playtime. A simple schedule could look like this:

- **7:15 am:** Wake up and go outside for potty

- **7:30 am:** Breakfast

- **8:00 am:** Playtime

- **8:15 am:** Outside for toilet

- **8:20 am:** Nap

- **10:15 am:** Outside for toilet

- **10:30 am:** Food and play

- **11:20 am:** Nap

And so on. You'll adjust the schedule as your puppy grows and requires fewer naps, but consistency is key in the early stages.

Potty Training in Apartments or Urban Areas

For those living in apartments or without easy access to a yard, potty training can still be successful with some adjustments. Consider using balcony grass patches or regularly taking your puppy to a designated spot outside. Make sure to stick to a schedule, and try to avoid long elevator waits or walks to the potty area—quick access will help reduce accidents.

Marking Behavior

Male dogs, in particular, may start to mark their territory inside the house. This isn't a potty training issue but rather a behavioral one. If your dog starts marking, distract them and take them outside immediately. If your dog isn't neutered, marking can be more common, but even neutered dogs may mark out of stress or anxiety. Clean marked areas thoroughly to prevent repeated marking.

Overall, house training takes time and patience, but with consistent efforts, it will soon become second nature for both you. Stick to a routine, offer plenty of praise, and keep an eye on your puppy's signals.

It might take a few months, but soon your puppy will be fully house-trained, and the challenges of potty training will be a distant memory!

Crate Training

Many people worry that using a crate might be cruel. If used properly, a crate is a place where your puppy will feel safe and happy - it will be his den. The main objective of your crate training is to teach him that the crate is his 'safe place' and that it belongs to him. Never use his crate as a 'sin bin'.

Using a crate will also bring with it a range of other benefits that will mean your life with your puppy can be as full and as engaging as possible - and it will allow him to be included in almost all of your activities, including vacations or holidays. Crate training is also often one of the best ways to help speed up house training.

The reason using the crate works for house training is that dogs don't like to mess where they sleep, and where they relax. Your puppy is unlikely to mess here, especially if you have crate trained him to view his crate as his safe place. What's more, if he is sleeping in his crate, he will do his very best to hold on.

This puts you in more control, because you will know where your puppy is, and what he might want to do when you open the door, or when he leaves his crate, especially if he has been sleeping.

Remember, you will always take him outside to toilet as soon as he wakes up and it is a good idea to do this every time he leaves the crate if he has been in there for 20-30 minutes or more, even if he has not been sleeping.

Crate training has lots of other benefits. Your dog will be able to travel with you more easily and safely. You can visit friends and family more easily because you can use the crate as his portable bed. It also means that you can go out knowing that you won't return to chewed furniture or a general mess (the chewing usually only occurs with puppies), and your dog can use the crate as his bed during the day and during the night.

In summary, the crate gives your dog and puppy somewhere safe to rest and to sleep. It helps him feel comfortable when you leave the house; he can feel safe in a new house or room that you are visiting, and it means that he can enjoy more of your life outside of the home if you need to travel.

It will also help his settle with a dog sitter or if he needs to go and stay away from home when you go on vacation.

Introducing your puppy to the crate

After picking your crate, and before he arrives home, add a blanket or something soft for your puppy to lie on. Ideally add an item that has a familiar scent and, if you are using a second-hand crate, make sure you wash it thoroughly to remove any scent from the previous owner.

If you are using a wire crate, have something like a sheet or a blanket that you can place on top of it as well as around the sides but don't cover up all four sides - make sure the front of the crate (where the door is) is left uncovered. This can help to make it feel more like a den, especially at night.

A puppy will not be used to being alone, and it will make his anxious, especially when he first arrives home. Having company around him will be important. This means that it's a good idea a the start, to place the crate in a room that is used by the rest of the household. This will help him get used to the crate without being separated from you and the rest of the family, and it will mean he doesn't feel alone and scared.

If you want to, you can put the crate into the room that you want him to use and then follow the steps below. Once you pick your room make sure that you also spend lots of time with him there.

When your puppy comes home, place his toys, and, if you have not already done so, add the scented item from his previous home, into the crate.

The first stage is to place some food around the crate. If he doesn't start moving towards the crate, or being curious about it all by himself, then entice him by calling him to the crate in a happy tone of voice, and by throwing tasty treats around and near the crate. Keep trying until he starts to come over to the crate and begins to feel comfortable around it.

The second stage is to slowly start moving the treats to the door, and then inside the crate. Give him lots of praise at all stages. Only start moving the treats inside the crate once he has started getting used to the outside edges of the crate. As he starts to enter the crate, don't close the door.

Keep playing the game and move the treats deeper into the crate. Let him enter and leave and explore if he wants to. You want to get him used to entering and leaving by himself.

It can take anything from 10 minutes to a few days, depending on his experience, to get him to go into his crate by himself. Keep the training sessions to between three and five minutes.

If, for any reason, your puppy is not responding to food or treats, then entice him with his favorite toy.

The third stage is to increase the length of time he spends in his crate. You can do this by feeding him in his crate, or you can put a Kong toy filled with treats into the cage, for him to play with.

If he is reluctant to go into the crate, put his food bowl beside the crate door, and then slowly move it into the crate until he eats at the back of the crate.

Once he is happy entering, leaving, and lingering for a few minutes in his crate, try to close the door. You can do this when he is eating, but one of the most effective ways is to give him the Kong stuffed with something he loves.

Wait until he starts to become engrossed in getting his food out of the Kong, then slowly close the door. If you close the door and he gets anxious or scared, immediately open the door.

If he does nothing, then wait for a few minutes before opening the door again.

Keep increasing the length of time before you open the door. You are aiming to reach 10 minutes. If he shows any signs of distress, if he is panting, whining, cowering, or showing any signs of aggression, then you will know you have increased the time too quickly.

Once your puppy is happy to stay in the crate for up to 10 minutes after eating or playing, then you will know that he is now likely to understand that this crate is his safe space.

The last stage of his crate training can now begin, and this is when you move out of sight, while he is in his crate with the door closed.

This is the stage when his toys and his Kong (filled with food, peanut butter, or soft cheese) will really help.

Put his toys in his crate, and close the door once he has entered. Stay beside the crate for around five minutes before moving quietly from the room and out of sight.

Once you are out of sight, turn around and come back to the side of the crate and sit beside it for 5 minutes. Gradually start to stay out of sight longer. Do this throughout the day but at different times. You will need to repeat the process several times.

If you hear any barking or whining, do not come back mid bark or mid whine. Try and find a gap, and this is when you return. You are aiming to increase the time you are out of sight to around 30 minutes.

Once this has been achieved, you can start leaving the house altogether. But remember to provide toys for his to play with, so that he does not get bored. Before leaving, make sure he has had a small meal and has been exercised, and remember to leave calmly without any fuss.

In terms of sleeping at night, you can put the crate in your bedroom at overnight in the early days. You only want to do this for a few days and not any longer.

When your puppy first arrives home, he will have been used to sleeping with his brothers and sisters, so letting him sleep in his crate in your room will help him settle in.

Once you put the crate into the room where he will normally spend the night, make sure to turn out the lights when you (and he) go to bed. You can leave a low-level one on if you like, but make sure it isn't bright.

This will also mean that if you need to take him out during the night, he will recognize that this is sleep time. And don't forget that if you need to take him out during the night, don't turn on all the lights.

Types of Crate

There are 3 main types of crate. A plastic crate (or box), a wire crate or cage, and one made of fabric. I use both a cage (in the house) and a fabric crate for travel, but I know many people who use a plastic crate. The choice is up to you. I use the fabric case as a travel carry case and use it as a den when we are staying away from home overnight.

What size of crate?

Unlike the crate's material, the size of the crate that you choose is important.

If the crate is too small, it will make your dog uncomfortable, and if it is too big, it can make your dog insecure. You need to know the height, width, and length of the crate.

The crate size will depend on both the weight and height of your puppy when he is fully grown.

The table below gives a general size and weight guide.

Finally, to save you from buying different crates as your puppy grows, you can section off a part of the crate with a separator to make it smaller when he is smaller.

Recommended crate sizes:

Small Dog Breeds 24″
Weight 11-25 lbs and 3″-17″ in height.

Medium Dog Breeds 30″
Weight 26-40 lbs and 18″-19″ in height.

Intermediate Dog Breeds 36″
Weight 41-70 lbs and 20″-22″ in height.

Large Dog Breeds 42″
Weight 71-90 lbs and 23″ - 26″ in height.

Chewing and Mouthing

Puppies not only chew but there is a period when they will use their mouths - a lot! This is called mouthing, and their tiny teeth are remarkably sharp.

They will grab your trouser legs or put their mouth around your hands - and their sharp teeth will take your breath away.

Puppies need to learn about different textures - and human skin is just one of the textures they need to learn about. They also need to understand how hard they can close their jaws, and when enough is enough. They can only learn this by doing it. If you have children then you need to be very aware of this.

Mouthing

All puppies will go through this phase. The aim of the game is to teach them about 'bite inhibition'.

This is something that puppies, who have come from a larger litter, will have learned a bit about, because they usually learn this through play with their litter mates (and socialization classes can help too).

If you have been around young puppies you will have heard squeals of outrage or pain, as they pushed each other over and mouthed at ears, paws, and anything they could get their tiny mouths around.

When one of the pups squeals, they also stop playing, but so does the protagonist who will often look as surprised as the pup that got a sharp tooth implanted into it. And, just a few moments later, they will be playing with each other again.

But, if you pay close attention, you will notice that the pup that got the painful nip was pretty eager to try this out on one of the other unsuspecting puppies.

This is just part-and-parcel of a puppy growing up and learning boundaries. But it doesn't make it easier or any less painful. However, over time, puppies learn to understand each other and know how hard a bite they can get away with. The screams of surprise between them always becomes less frequent.

Puppies are most likely to try and mouth you when you are playing with them, tickling their tummy, or petting them.

Not surprisingly, the best way to deal with mouthing is to behave like a puppy.

First of all - it's important to let your puppy mouth you.

Let him have your hand. When he closes his mouth too hard, and his sharp teeth become painful, squeal like a puppy or use the word "stop" and immediately stop playing with him. Let your hand go limp so that it is no fun to play with.

This should stop your puppy for a moment or two. He will be just as surprised as you. When he relaxes his mouth and stops, praise him. Then let him have your hand again.

He will go too far quite a few times, so just keep repeating over a 15- or 20-minute time period until he learns how hard he can close his mouth without hurting you.

If your squealing and "stop" doesn't work, then put him on the "naughty step" so to speak. Stop playing with him for 30 seconds or so. After this, start playing with him again.

If he does it again, then repeat, and if this still doesn't work, then move away from him as soon as he mouths you and you feel that nip.

As the hard biting stops, you will want to continue teaching him as he moves his mouthing levels down from sore to moderate. Slowly teaching him not to mouth at all.

Eventually, he will know exactly the level of pressure that he can safely apply when he is playing.

Whatever you do, don't hit your puppy for mouthing. This will only make him play harder, but it may also cause him to fear you.

Remember not to jerk your hands away from your puppy when he starts mouthing you. He will think this is a part of the game and it can make him more likely to lunge forward. Likewise, don't wave your hands in front of his face for the same reason - he will think that this is a game too.

Once you have done this, he will finally know not to mouth at all on human skin, and to let you pet him without being mouthed.

When your puppy tries to mouth you when you are petting them, distract him by giving him a treat or a chew toy. I ended up using a tug toy. Wave it in front of him and just said, "Play Tug."

One last thing to bear in mind. Like all toddlers, puppies can have tantrums. His body will be stiffer, and his mouth might be tighter around the lips. If you notice this while you are playing with your puppy, just stop the play.

Don't squeal if he bites you (it will be harder than normal). If you are holding him, stop playing but continue to hold him for a few seconds, then let him go.

Don't make him afraid of you, you just want him to know that he has gone too far. If you notice that your puppy continues to have tantrums, you will need to get more help from a professional.

Chewing

Most dogs like to chew, and some breeds are more likely to chew than others. For example, Labradors and Staffordshire Bull Terriers tend to have a stronger desire to chew. Because Golden-doodles, like their poodle ancestry, are intelligent with moderate-to-high energy, they need a lot of mental stimulation and if they are bored, they will be inclined to chew.

All puppies enjoy and need to chew. They do this to explore their environment and understand the texture of things; they don't have hands, and they like to pick things up. So the only way that he can explore is to use his mouth.

All puppies go through the teething phase which also causes chewing. Depending on your puppy, he will start to experience discomfort in his mouth as his teething process gets underway anywhere between four and eight months. He will chew to help remove his baby teeth, and he will chew to help with the pain of his adult teeth erupting in his gums.

• 4 Months old - the incisors begin to grow in
• 5 months old - the canine teeth begin to grow in
• 6 months old - the molars begin to grow in
• By 8 months old, a puppy should have all teeth ascended and stop teething. Some Goldendoodles will be later than this and teething may last a bit longer.

As your puppy starts to reach adolescence, his chewing is going to get worse. There are two possible reasons for this.

It is around now that he will tend to get easily bored so try to find new games (especially mental exercise games) and games to keep him occupied.

It is also around this time that his adult teeth are settling into the jaw, which can be uncomfortable for some dogs.

Whatever the reason, and it might be both of the above reasons, your puppy is going to chew. It can be furniture, especially the legs of tables, the sides of the sofa, shoes, wallets, and spectacles.

You will need to teach everyone in your household to put their shoes out of reach, and preferably out of sight, along with any toys that have different textures.

There will be the favored chew items. Puppies love shoes - they are just about the right consistency of hard and soft making them perfect for exploring different textures. Much the same as furniture too.

Don't forget that your puppy might chew all of his life but it will never be as bad as that first year. (Dogs also chew because it relaxes them and it's a calming activity - and they enjoy it).

Here are some chew toys and tips that might help

- Try and change your dog's chew toys regularly by rotating them every few days. This will prevent him from getting bored and prevent him from looking for something else to chew that might look more interesting.
- Remove anything that you don't want him to chew and keep everything well out of reach. This includes TV remote controls or spectacles - move them to higher ground, well out of reach.
- If you find your puppy chewing on something that is not allowed, don't punish him or shout at him. This will only make him anxious. Instead, simply distract his attention and then direct him to a chew toy that you want him to play with. When he starts to play with it, make a fuss of him.
- Don't forget to remove anything dangerous to your puppy when he cannot be supervised. This includes some types of household plants (see below) that are poisonous to dogs. And watch out for wires that run along the floor.
- Many hard plastic toys are not made for dog chewing. The best chew toys are made of the type of hard rubber that you get with your Kong. You can also consider activity balls (like Kong's, you can place kibble, cheese spread, peanut butter, or other treats). Ropes are also

good but avoid nylon or anything that he can pull apart into a string.

- Chews such as dental chews or edible chews can distract your puppy - but they can be eaten quite quickly. Test which chews your puppy likes the most and which ones last the longest.
- Keep all house plants well out of reach, especially the ones that are poisonous to dogs. For example Cyclamen, Poinsettia, some Lilly's, Oleander, Brunfelsia, Aloe, Amaryllis (bulbs), Azalea, Cyclamen, Water Hemlock. You can find a list on the DogsTrust website.

Basic Training

Now it's time to talk about the training that you might be more familiar with and you can begin training some cues in the house and in the garden before you start taking your puppy outside for walks. It is always a good idea to cover the basics at home.

First of all you need to have a few items and systems in place.

Treats

Treats are the mainstay of dog training at the puppy stage, but you should also introduce other rewards such as toys and praise as the training progresses. In a few cases dogs can prefer toys to treats.

Some people cut up hot dogs, while some trainers make liver cake, some dogs love carrots, and others use a store bought dog treat. One of the simplest things to do is to grab a handful of his kibble and use this as a dog training treat. You will need a selection of 3 or 4 different treats because you will want to adopt a value-reward system.

Value-Reward System

A value-reward approach means that you will reward a type of treat based on how difficult the task is that you are asking your puppy to do. Kibble, for example, is often not as highly valued as cheese or a piece of hot dog or a carrot. This means that your puppy will like kibble, but he will like a hot dog more and he will love a small bit of cheese, and he will adore a little bit of liver cake.

In this example, he would get what he loves most when he accomplishes something difficult or that he has never done before. You will then use this knowledge to reward based on difficulty, the more difficult the higher the reward value.

This allows you to reward on value depending on what you want him to do. You will use this for recall training too - the faster he returns the higher the value of reward. It means that you can use the treat (and later, the reward) that matches his effort.

For example, if he absolutely loves cheese then save this as a special treat when he does something for the first few times. If he has already learned to sit, then offer him kibble when he sits. Try not to move from high value to low value as soon as he learns to sit, gradually move down the value chain to kibble. This process can also increase the connection between you and your puppy. Don't forget that you will be praising him all the time.

There are a few reasons that treats might not work. They might not be tasty enough, he might be too stressed or he might get his treats all the time so he doesn't realize what the reward means - this is known as over-reinforcement. It's also possible that your puppy might not be hungry. Try and train him on an empty stomach but not right before he is due to be fed - if a puppy is too hungry then all that his mind will be concentrating on is food and he won't be able to concentrate on his training.

Over reinforcement, which simply means using treats too often, is common. This can be hard to get right but using the value reward system can help. Over-time, rather than getting kibble for example he will get lots of praise and no treat, or his treat might be to do something he loves (play or get the ball) as well as lots of praise.

Remember, you are eventually aiming to have the desired behavior with no treats (and you won't always be able to have a treat in your hand.)

Harness

Collars and choke collars are no longer thought to be good for dogs. They can be worn in the house but a harness should be used for training - especially leash and recall. Training is all about trust, and restrictive items just won't build the trust you are looking for.

Leash

Avoid using a flexible leash. They won't give you the control that you need and they get tangled up in legs, including yours, or someone else's. Ideally, you have a long-leash (around 25ft-30ft in length). This is known as a long-line. You will also want a shorter training leash of around 4ft and you can use this as his day-leash or 'normal' leash.

Whistles and Clickers

Almost all leash training will involve using a clicker but you can train with and without a clicker. Whistles are great for recall especially for dog breeds that like to explore and can be good for your Goldendoodle.

With clicker training, the click must always be followed with a reward, for example, click-treat. This is known as the primary and secondary enforcer.

Toys

You are going to use your puppy's toys during recall training. You are aiming to get him to leave a toy and come to you when he is called. You will have a treat so that he sees the value of leaving his toy and coming to you instead.

Basic Training

You can begin basic training over the first few weeks that your puppy is home by teaching him the basic commands that you will use throughout his life.

Always keep the training sessions to between 5 and 10 minutes. If he comes up against something he can't do, then return to something that he can do.

You always want him to enjoy the training session so if he gets stuck, take him back a step so that, at the end of the session as well as during it, he is happy and receives his praise and reward - it is important to end the session on a positive note.

I will mention using hand signals during some of the training in the following pages, and you should try to use this type of training as much as you can, rather than only verbal cues. Use both if you don't feel comfortable with only hand signals.

Reinforcement (a part of operant conditioning) and using body language rather than verbal cues is now considered as the foundation for good dog training. Reinforcement is rewarding without a treat i.e. by using praise and offering your puppy something else he loves (a toy or to go and play).

Getting to know his name

Always reward your puppy when he responds to his name. It doesn't matter how or why he responds to his name, it only matters that he does, and you need to reward his for doing so. You will start to do this as soon as he arrives home.

Whenever you say his name and he looks at you, even if it was an accidental look, reward him.

Don't ever be tempted to use his name as punishment because he won't understand the tone of voice and anger in relation to your use of his name.

Paying Attention

The next stage is to teach him to look at you and you will do this before you start taking your puppy outdoors for walks. I know dogs that, to this day, don't make eye contact with their owner. It is an often overlooked training activity and yet it is a hidden gem in terms of getting your puppy, and later your grown-up dog's, attention and it will make his training much easier.

It will mean that, even if your puppy starts to get engrossed or fixated on something, you can get his attention back to you, and you can change his focus to you, to stop him doing whatever it was that he was doing. I find this particularly useful for leash training.

To do this he needs to want to pay attention to you.

You will already have started training him to look at you during the period you were teaching him his name, but now you want to actively encourage it and to repeat the process in many different locations and environments. You will say his name, he needs to look at you and as soon as he makes eye contact, then you can reward him with click-treat, or with praise and reward, and the reward could be a treat or to play with a toy.

A game is the best way to train your Poodle puppy to look at you.

To play the game, sit down with your puppy with a handful of treats in your pocket. Make sure that you are sitting so that you are close to him, but so that he needs to look up to see your eyes.

Take out a treat and get his attention. Place the treat between your eyes. Your puppy will follow the treat all the way to your head and eyes. As soon as there is eye-contact, even briefly, give him the treat.

In the beginning, the eye contact might be an accident on his part but that's okay. If he gets rewarded for it, he will soon learn. Keep repeating until he always has eye contact with you. If he doesn't look at you at first, then help his find your eyes so that he knows what he is supposed to do.

Once he knows what the game is and is responding in the way that you want, start putting the treat behind your head or neck and so that he can't see the treat. Again, as soon as there is eye contact - but not before - give him the treat.

The next part of this game is to start using his name. Do exactly the same process but as you place the treat between your eyes, say his name. You will need to do all this quite quickly to link the eye contact with the name call and his reward but he will get there.

He now knows that when you say his name you want him to look at you, and he will want to pay attention to you because there will be a reward coming!

The Fundamental Cues

You will begin teaching your puppy what you mean by the recall cue. I will use the example of 'come'. The important part is to always use the same word and use it only when you want him to come to you.

Don't mix it into other cues. This one word means one thing, and one thing only - to come to you.

You will adopt this rule for all his cues. Make sure each one is unique to the action expected and can't be confused with other cues. For example, don't use 'come here' if 'here' is used as another cue that needs a different action.

Start your training in the house then move to enclosed areas with few distractions.

Sit

There are a few ways to teach your puppy to sit, but I have used this one to the best effect.

Sit down beside your puppy holding a treat, then put the treat in front of his nose, slowly lifting it above his head. As he tilts his head up to follow the treat, he is likely to sit as he tries to reach the treat. Notice you hand movement (you hand will tilt up slightly as he sits and reaches for his treat).

Say the word 'sit' just before his bottom touches the ground. Then, as soon as his bottom touches the ground, reward him with the treat. Your puppy is learning the word sit but also starting to recognize your hand signal i.e. the movement of your arm and hand.

Keep doing this, eventually removing the treat from your hand but using your hand as a signal or cue to get him to sit, and saying the word 'sit' as you raise your hand to the sitting position. Always reward him as soon as he sits down.

Don't try to push his bottom to the ground to get him to sit - it rarely works.

Lie Down

For some reason, this is the fastest command to teach when you do it like this, and your puppy will be lying down within one training session.

Simply take out his treat and hold it to his nose, then move it down slowly to the floor (you can say 'Lie' at this point too rather than wait until later in training). Slide the treat on the floor away from him. He will start to move down. Again, notice your arm and had action as you do this as you slowly, move your arm backwards with you fingers 'pointing' to the floor (or, in the early stages, on the floor).

As soon as he is almost down (he won't lie down right away, and his bottom is likely to remain in mid-air), gave him the treat.

Keep doing this and getting him to move further into the lie position (you can keep dragging the treat towards you on the floor as this can often help).

Reward and praise him each time. Eventually, you will only give him the treat when he is fully down. By now, he will be used to your hand moving down and hearing the phrase 'Lie'.

Training sit-stay

To teach your dog to stay, first of all, ask him to sit. Then hold up your hand so that your palm is straight in front of him and directed towards his face (but not in any kind of threatening way).

Take a step backward so that you are facing him and with your palm facing him and say 'stay'. If he stays for even a few seconds, come back to him and reward him.

Do this a few times and then take a few more steps backward increasing the distance, then walk back to his and reward him. Keep repeating moving further away.

Your puppy is learning that not only is he getting rewarded but that you come back to him. Start to move to different positions so that you are to each side and eventually behind him. If he gets up, just move back to him and give him praise then try again.

You will need to repeat this in several different locations aeon the house and in the garden. As he starts to get better at this, begin to introduce him to areas with more distractions, or create distractions like more people of other dogs he knows, and start moving behind objects so that he can't see you. Try and do this everywhere you go.

Every time after that, when your puppy sits try and remember to praise/reward his as he will build this into a behavior default. One that he will enjoy, feels safe with, and knows will bring praise/reward.

The 'come' cue

I know of someone who began basic recall in their hallway, which was ideal for ensuring their puppy was set up for success during the early training because there were limited directional options, and little distraction. This is important. Remember that you want to ensure that your puppy always succeeds and this might mean you need to adapt things to make sure that he can succeed through each step of his training.

Once you have decided on your location, show your puppy his favorite treat or toy, and as he comes towards you to get his toy or treat (don't ask his to come to you, let him do it by himself), praise him and reward him as he reaches you. Do this a few times.

Once again, add some distraction. One fun way to do this is to have other family members or friends in a room with you. As you walk towards them and he starts to get interested in this curious and fun distraction, quickly run away and call him so that he chases you.

Encourage him to catch up and when he does, he will of course get his treat and probably a big cuddle as an extra reward.

Like many of the training games you can play with him, mix them up so that he doesn't always know what to expect. It will keep him even more interested in what you are about to get up to next. And don't forget to get other family members to lead the training too.

After a few times of playing this game, start to add in his cue so that he gets used to it. As he starts coming towards you to get his toy (and ideally looks at you), add in the cue you have chosen. In my example, 'Come'.

Combine sit, stay and come

Finally, combine the 'come' cue with the 'sit and stay' cue.

Ask your puppy to sit, and then ask him to stay and try to remember to use your use visual hand cue.

Walk backwards a few steps while facing your puppy - you can keep holding your hand up in the stay position as your walk away.

The difference now is that you want him to come to you following the sit-stay. If he stays for just a few seconds, ask him to come and give him a treat when he comes to you.

Keep repeating this and do it at the start of every training session. As he starts to get good at this, start to move further and further away and eventually try walking away with your back to his.

Like all of his training, build up the distance and the distractions to this game - but if you go too far and he starts to come towards you too soon, just go back a few steps to the point at which it was working and then keep trying to build the distance.

The next stage is to go outside but not for a 'proper' walk just yet. You can go for a walk on-leash but not off-leash.

Summary and the 10 steps for basic recall

1. Decide on your location (hallway, kitchen, etc) - and later, vary the location
2. Show your puppy his favorite toy or a treat but don't call him, let him come to you

3. When he gets to you give him the treat along with praise
4. Repeat
5. Start adding your recall cue ('come', visual cue or whistle) as he starts coming towards you
6. Reward him when he gets to you
7. Repeat steps 5 and 6
8. When he comes to you give him the treat then ask him to sit and give his another treat
9. Repeat this until he knows what to do
10. Ask him to sit and stay, walk away from him (initially walking backwards so that you are facing him) and then use his cue to come to you
11. When he gets to you give him the treat along with praise
12. Repeat the recall and sit and stay in other locations and start to add in distractions

Leash training

You can start putting his lead on in the house so that he gets used to it. As soon as his leash is clipped on, give him a treat. Have another treat in your hand and use this to get him to walk beside you.

To do this, hold the treat just in front of his nose, loosely cupped in your hand, so that your palm is facing his nose with your arm hanging down beside you. Once again, notice your had position as you do this - this will be what he will get to know as the 'heel' cue.

He will move towards your hand as you start taking a few steps forward which makes him move and walk along beside you. Build this up slowly and for no more than 5 minutes at a time at the start.

Eventually, walk a few paces, then turn in the opposite direction getting him to follow you (more specifically, following your hand!).

Repeat this process of walking a few steps and turning.

By this stage, your puppy will know sit, stay, come and will be able to walk beside you (on the leash). We will no talk about off leash and for this we need to train recall.

Recall Training

In this chapter we will outline the main training you will start doing with your puppy as you prepare, and then, start taking him out for walks.

Dogs train better when they are making their own choices. You want him to want to make the choice to come to you, when you ask him. This means that you must never be angry when he comes back to you, no matter how long it has taken.

You are aiming to have your dog return to you on cue no matter how many other exciting things are going on around him. You can only achieve this if you are more interesting than whatever else he is doing, and if he is listening and paying attention to you.

In summary, you want him to stop what he is doing; you want him to look at you, and you want him to come to you on cue.

Introducing the recall cue

Most people use the word 'come' or 'here' as their vocal cue for their recall. Some might use a whistle or a visual cue, and often all 3 at different times. Once you have decided on the word you want to use, then you must keep it. Consistency is vital for your dog to understand what you mean.

Start using this cue early - and it will be the come cue that you used in the last chapter as part of basic training. You will use this cue for many reasons. When you want him to come for his dinner, when you are going to give him a big cuddle or play with him. The outcomes of the 'come' cue for him in these examples, means that when he hears the word and responds correctly, he feels great because he gets something he loves and he gets lots of praise from you. In dog training language, he is building a positive association with the word. You want this feeling (and his response to your cue) to continue when he is playing away from you.

Try to build in hand signals too - I tend to open my arms as a visual cue to come.

Like most training sessions, keep the training to around 10 minutes and watch out for any signs that he is getting stressed (quick head movements, grabbing the treat/food, ears flat) and try not to get him over-excited.

If your puppy is a part of a household then get all members involved in the training too. Don't forget to ask him to do some-thing you know he can do at the end of the training so that it ends in success. You want him to enjoy this training.

You will have already introduced him to training at home including the basic 'sit', 'stay, and 'come' cues. You will now begin leash and recall training in preparation for his daily walks and exercise in the park.

You won't let him off leash outside in an unenclosed area until you are happy that he will return to you.

To do this you need to introduce him to different locations and train him in these locations - different rooms in the house, different areas of the garden or different areas of an enclosed area. You will then introduce lots of distractions as the training develops - a toy, another person, another dog that you know (and that you know is vaccinated) etc and you will keep doing the training exercises with all these distractions present.

You are aiming to get him to always pay attention to you and to always return to you despite any exciting activity or scents that he might be interested in - and if he can get used to this in a safe garden then he will be familiar with what to do once he gets to the park.

When it comes to recall, you should wait until his recall is up to about 70%-80% before you start adding the distraction element of his recall training.

Sit Stay Release

By this stage (by the time you are going for outside walks) you will have trained your puppy to 'sit' and will have practiced some 'stay' and 'come' in the home or garden, along with walking beside you (on or off leash). We have covered this earlier.

You will now start to use the sit cue for a variety of reasons. In the car, when you go to the door, when you are at a crosswalk, and so on. This means you need to train him to sit but you also need to let him know when it's okay to move forward.

To do this, start by having him on his leash. Get him to sit (and reward) then decide on your cue for 'let's go' this can be 'let's go' or 'ok go' or whatever you choose. Say your cue and move a few steps and praise him, ask him to sit and reward.

Begin with short distances (a few steps) to get him used to the 'ok go' cue. Repeat the process of 'sit', reward 'ok go' reward, walk a few steps then repeat. This is known as the release cue.

This can mean that the release cue is seen as a reward too because when he comes back he then gets to go and have fun again. It also means that he will learn that coming back doesn't mean the end of the play.

Finally, some trainers consider recall to include holding your puppy's collar when he returns as full recall and they use it before the release cue. The puppy comes back, he sits and the collar is taken then the reward is given. This is followed by the release cue.

Some are happy with only the sit. This really is up to you but I prefer the collar hold as it gives you more control should you ever need it.

Training Outside

Training for recall outside of the house is vital. It is here that he is going to find the most distractions. You must make sure that the area you choose is fully enclosed. Just like the early days of house training, you will start with very few distractions.

This is when you are going to work with the clicker and training leads and when you will start working out the value that he attaches to each of his different treats (if you haven't already done so).

Don't train him for too long. Pay attention if he looks like he is getting bored and stop the training and start again the next day.

Getting started

To get started, put your puppy in his harness and on his training leash. Just like the early indoor training, you can start with rewarding an action with no other cues, to get him used to the long-line and outdoor training. He will know what to do quickly, because he has already been trained indoors.

The difference now is that you are going to place something he might want to eat or might want to get (a toy), a short distance away from him, and within the length of the leash, or just a bit further away. You are now introducing something he wants to get to but that is away from you.

As he goes towards the object or the treat (but not too tasty), tighten his leash and say his name then the cue e.g., Barney 'come'. As soon as he turns and comes (even if it's only a step or two) reward and praise him.

If you are using a clicker, you will click as soon as he turns. Aim to have an even tastier treat for him than the one he was going towards. You want to increase the value of the treats the more you want him to do something, so that he prefers to choose that tastier treat.

By having the leash on him, you can also gently encourage him to come towards you to get his reward if you need to. The leash helps you have a bit of control over this recall in the early stages as he continues to establish the cue 'come' outside of the house, and where he will want to explore more.

You will also play on the training leash and long line. Give him a few treats then run forward or backward a few steps and say 'Bailey, Come!' in a playful voice while holding a treat out at the height of his nose (so that all of his feet are on the ground) and as he reaches you give him the treat.

You can extend this game to add the sit. As he reaches you to get his treat, move the treat up in front of his nose, so that he is forced back into the sit position to get his treat. In this way the come and sit are the same cue which means when you ask him to come, he will come to you and sit without being asked to sit.

You can, and should start practicing this as soon as you can. Puppies learn most up to the age of 18 weeks.

Using the long-line

The next step for recall training is to have him move further away from you, and for him to return when he hears his cue. Good recall means he does this all the time. If he is not, then he is not ready, and you won't want to risk letting him off-leash.

You don't need to use the long-line but it can be really helpful and, if you can, I would recommend it. Practice this in a garden if you can, and, in the beginning, have no other distractions. The aim is get familiar with working with the long line and checking and testing that your training is working.

Working with the Long-line

Hold the end of the line in your right hand (if you are right handed) so that you have it tightly held. Then wrap the length of the line into loops so that you can slowly release the line over the front of your body, feeding it through your left hand.

The 'feeder' in your left hand is acting as your dog leash controlling the delivery of the line, and it is attached to his harness. This means you can slowly release the line through your left hand, to allow your puppy to move away from you, or clamp it closed (gently) to slow or stop the release of the line. Once you are comfortable you can start the training.

Slowly move in a circle on the same spot so that he is running around you, loosening the line so that he can move away from you, and then call him back to you. Just get him used to the leash and watching you, and knowing that he gets a reward when he comes back.

You can then add a game (and later you can play this off-leash too), by throwing a treat away from you, and letting your puppy go towards the treat.

Once he has eaten his treat, call his name to get his attention, wait until he looks at you (click), 'come' (cue), and when he comes to you (praise/reward). Then throw another treat in a different direction so that he is constantly running away and towards you in a fun game.

When you need to tighten or 'pull' the line to encourage him to come back on his cue, move or lean forward rather than move against him, and gently make the line shorter. This allows you to be in control of your puppy whilst letting him return without feeling 'pulled'.

The final part is to wait until he is preoccupied with something and is not looking at you. Get his attention and ask him to come. If he comes then praise and reward. If he doesn't come, just walk to him and show him all the treats you have, and then walk away from him.

He is likely to follow you to try and get a treat. Just ignore him. As soon as he isn't right beside you, ask him to come to you. When he does, give his lots of praise and a favorite treat. It won't take long for him to realise that coming is much better than not coming.

The next step is to repeat the indoor sit stay come training in the outdoor environment. Just as you did indoors get your puppy to sit-stay and then move away from him while still facing him and then ask him to 'come'. e.g., 'Bailey, come'. Slowly build the distance all the while using the long line.

The next two steps are new, and before you can try off-leash outdoor you want to introduce the 'let's go' or 'let's play' cue which combines the sit-stay.

Ask him to sit-stay beside you, then use your release cue, 'let's go', and start walking. As he moves away and then moves ahead of you, call him back to you (click on a turn of the head towards you), as he starts coming towards you, you might want to encourage him, reward him when he gets to you, then ask him to sit and reward again.

Off-leash

The last step is to practice off-leash - again, you will do this in a space that is enclosed and where he will be safe. Let him wander away from you and then call him to you using your cue. Try and keep his attention on you as he comes to you - make a noise or hold your arms open - you want him to be focused on you. And don't forget to have his reward ready.

Don't keep repeating the cue or start raising your voice if he doesn't come. This will confuse him, and he won't be able to understand what his cue word is, eventually tuning it out which means he just won't hear it.

If you raise your voice and sound annoyed he won't think that coming to you is going to be lots of fun. Eventually, it could have the opposite effect, and he won't want to come at all.

The best way to train your puppy is using random and variable reinforcement. All this means is that over time change how often he gets a treat for the same behavior, so that he is hoping for it each time (don't wait too long to reward as you start to reduce the level of treats) and change the value of the treat (for a really good response).

If you want to, you can measure the average response time for recall (either daily or per 12 returns, etc.) so that when he comes back faster, he gets a super tasty treat. This is the most effective way to train your puppy to become addicted to coming back to you.

One last trick - if your puppy has taken a while to return on cue then, when he arrives, show him the treat and put it back in your pocket. As he moves away ask him to 'come' and, when he gets to you, give him his treat. This will help him learn that acting right away gets the reward.

Using a Clicker

Clicker training is useful when you want to mark the correct behavior of your puppy at the exact moment that he starts to respond. If you are doing click-reward then it must always be followed by a reward, but the reward and the timing of the reward varies.

In the beginning, all you need to do is get your puppy used to the click-reward (at the start you will use a treat). Keep repeating click-treat. He doesn't have to do anything at this stage as you are just getting him used to the clicker marker which means a reward is coming.

Slowly reduce the time between the click and the treat and vary the gaps - he will still expect the treat and he will know that it is coming, but that it might not happen right away.

Once he gets good at this, you will be able to click without the treat, and vary the reinforcement by using his favorite toy or a quick game that he likes.

For example, when you call his name and he begins to start coming towards you, you can click so that he knows a reward is coming. It helps to keep him motivated to come all the way back to you in the expectation of a good time when he gets there.

Below is how clicker training fits in to the training as well as how it fit in to recall. If you are training without a clicker just ignore the click-marker.

Recall Summary with the Clicker

The general process for recall training is as follows:

1. Call your dog (use your 'come' cue)
2. When he comes ask his to "Sit" (cue). Take his collar and praise his and reward
3. Release his "Ok Go" (cue)

The complete process would look like this (with the click timing included):

1. **Get your puppy to come to you**. Start by throwing a treat away from you then throw a treat at your feet. Reward every time your puppy comes back to you for any reason. You can add the click with your clicker to mark as soon as he turns towards you.

2. **Add a cue** . As your puppy turns towards you, again, this is for any reason, add your recall cue and your click (if you are using a clicker to mark or capture the behavior). The recall cue can be 'come', 'here' or a whistle - either your own whistle or use a plastic one.

3. **As you are walking on the leash vary the length.** Every time he looks towards you, click and then add the recall cue (and don't forget the reward). Practice at different locations and over different distances before you move to the next step.

4. **You will now cue him to look and come to you.** With your puppy walking in front of you say (or whistle) your cue, as he turns towards you add the click marker. Practice by varying the distance and the speed the dog is moving away. When he returns to you reward.

5. **If you want to add a sit** then this is when you will add it to your training. When he arrives back to you use your sit cue to get him to sit. As soon as he sits add a click and then the reward.

6. **Add a collar hold.** You can train this separately or you can add it into the recall process here. When he has arrived back and sits, lean in and take hold of his collar - as you do this use your clicker to mark then reward.

Once he is good and is succeeding with steps 1 to 6 you can start adding in distractions.

Distractions

You will start with low-level distractions and build them up to higher-value distractions.

Distractions might be kibble, bread, eggs, cheese, meat, and toys (again in order of least to most favorite).

As he moves towards the distraction e.g., the bread, start your recall cue, and the reward process above (if you are using a clicker just add the click marker). If he fails then reduce the value of the distraction you are tempting him with until he is succeeding.

In terms of what other distractions might be, it doesn't need to be his favourite treats but they are a good place to start. You can then add a dog he knows, a dog he doesn't know (high-value distraction), someone he knows, a group of people, a jogger, a bicycle, an old scent, and the high-value new scent (a squirrel that you have noticed running up a tree).

Try and remember to complete a sequence. Try to always have your dog notice you (click), come to you (encouragement), arrive (treat), sit (treat), collar hold (treat), 'go play' (reward). This is much more rewarding than 'come', treat, end of the game.

By continuing to reward after he comes back to you, by rewarding the sit, collar hold and then releasing with a 'go play' cue, he will have the expectation of more exciting things to come than if the rewards ended with the return cue only.

He also knows that he can return to playing if he comes back to you and also receives all of his rewards. Don't forget that the 'go play' cue is a reward in itself.

This will become even more useful once you start going outdoors to parks and longer walks where there are even more exciting distractions and ones that you are not in control of.

Proofing

Proofing is when you want to 'prove' that the training has worked and you will need to do this before you let your puppy off-leash.

To do this, you will create distractions and then aim to get his to come to you on cue as you have done above but you are testing once more.

Try and arrange a play-date with at least one other dog and then while he is playing with it (and still on the long-line) call him to you. Make sure you have a very tasty treat and be full of praise when he comes to you.

Once he comes to you and receives his reward he is then released to the cue, such as 'let's go', to play again. As already mentioned, this particular activity is also useful to teach him that coming to you doesn't mean the end of the playtime.

The last step is to practice off-leash - again, you will do this in a space that is enclosed and where he will be safe. Simply let him wander away from you and then call him to you using your cue. Be exciting and have a treat ready for him.

Don't keep repeating the cue if he doesn't come and don't raise your voice to a shout (or scream). This will confuse him and he won't be able to understand what his cue word is. If you raise your voice, he won't think that coming to you is going to be lots of fun, and he won't want to come at all.

If he isn't coming to you as you go through all the training then go back to the long line until you are sure he understands what you are asking him to do.

Emergency stop

Training for an emergency stop can save your dog's life. It is also quite easy to train especially once you have been working on recall training.

First of all, you will want to use a specific cue. This can be any word but, again, it can only have one meaning. The most common word that is used is 'Stop'.

To begin with, have your puppy sitting in front of you and have a treat in your hand. If your puppy is not food orientated try using one of his toys.

Take a step back, put your arm in the air as if you are trying to stop the traffic. This is important as it is more likely that your emergency stop signal will be visual and not sound-based because your dog is likely to be a distance away from you.

Raise your arm with the treat in your hand, say the word 'Stop', and then throw the treat over your dog's head towards his rear so that the treat falls behind him or just beside him. You want to make sure that your dog needs to turn around to get the treat.

As he starts to return to you, repeat by putting your arm in the air, saying 'Stop' and throwing another treat over his head. This will force him to stop to turn around to get the treat.

You will notice that he starts to pay attention to you and your hand, which is what you want him to do.

Once he is paying attention, stopping and turning to get the treat as you raise your arm, you can think about increasing the distance of your throw. If there are any problems with the next step return to this previous stage.

Keep throwing the treat a bit further away so that there is a bigger distance between you both, so that when you say 'Stop', put your arm in the air, and throw the treat over his head, he is not close to you. This is how you can build up the long-distance emergency stop.

Try to make sure the treat doesn't land in front of him because you want him to turn around to get the treat. You want him to do this because it stops his forward movement. Keep building up the distance and repeating the exercise.

The aim is to reach the point where, with your arm in the air, you say Stop, he looks towards you and stops. If he starts to come towards you, go back to the first step and reinforce the Stop when he is right in front of you.

If your dog is a fast learner it may take a few days but this can take a few weeks so just be patient.

The very last step is when you don't throw the treat at the end but, instead, you walk towards him to give him the reward. This is because, if you are in a park and he is far away, you won't be able to throw a treat behind him but you want him to know that a reward is coming.

Recall: What not to do

- If your dog does not return to you when you call him simply go and retrieve him and put him on his leash. Don't be angry with him, simply put him on the leash, and move him away from whatever it is that is distracting him.
- Don't keep calling the same cue over and over again. For example, if he does not come when you call and you keep repeating the cue louder and louder the cue itself will lose its value and your puppy will simply tune it out as noise. If your cue isn't working then choose a new one and train your puppy to know what it is.
- Don't have only one person training him if he lives with other family members. If your puppy is a family dog then everyone needs to be involved in the training, and everyone needs to use the same cues. Ideally, everyone should be involved in the daily training, even for just a few minutes.
- Never punish your puppy when he fails. This is particularly important with recall (and with separation anxiety). If you get angry with them, or punish them, when they finally return to you after not coming back right away, all they will learn is that coming back to you is not a good experience and that it has negative consequences. All this will do is make his recall worse, not better.

- Don't use the "come" cue if your dog if fully focused on something else and is unlikely to 'hear' you. In this case, use his name to get his attention and to check that he can hear you (does he react by turning slightly towards you or twitch his ear). If he does, then use his "come" cue. If he is far away, you can use a whistle or whistle yourself, and if he can see you use your hand signal. If he does not 'come' you know he is not fully trained so re-start the training to the point he was succeeding, and build it up again from there.
- Finally, do no use the recall cue for things they might not like doing. For example, don't associate it with a bath, or getting groomed, or having a tick removed if he doesn't like these things.

Going to the Park

When you're ready to take your Goldendoodle to the park, you'll encounter lots of new distractions. Goldendoodles are highly social and excitable dogs, and keeping their attention on you will require some planning.

Since the environment will be more stimulating, make sure that you have higher-value treats than the ones you've been using indoors or in enclosed spaces. Goldendoodles tend to be naturally curious and energetic, so returning to you might be more challenging when they're distracted by new sights, smells, and other dogs.

Recall throughout the walk is key so don't call your dog back only at the end of the walk, or they might associate recall with the end of playtime. Instead, practice recall several times during your outing, rewarding them each time they come back to you.

Because Goldendoodles are very smart, they can also get bored if everything is too predictable. To keep them motivated, vary the treats so they stay excited, knowing something really tasty is coming their way and vary the timing of when you give the treat— sometimes offer it immediately, and other times after a few seconds. This helps maintain their focus and teaches them to stay attentive, without expecting an instant reward every time they return to you.

Don't forget to adjust how you reward him based on how quickly he responds to your recall command. If he hesitates or takes his time, let him sniff the treat but don't give it immediately. Instead, call him again, and when he turn around quickly and comes back to you, that's when you give the treat and lots of praise.

In the early stages, even if your pup takes longer, still give him a small reward rather than withholding it completely. This means that he won't feel discouraged from returning , even if he was slower.

Don't forget to keep it fun and rewarding - it means that your Goldendoodle will see coming back to you as something exciting, not a sign that playtime is over.

At the end of the walk, again, make extra sure that returning to you is fun. Play a quick game, offer an extra special treat, or give them lots of praise. This reinforces the idea that returning to you is always enjoyable and something to look forward to, even when it's time to leave the park.

It's a great idea to start with a long training line when you first take them to the park. This gives your dog more freedom to explore but allows you to maintain control. You can drop the line and let them run, but if they go too far, simply stand on the line to stop them. This method is far easier than trying to grab a shorter leash if they get distracted and run off.

As you begin to explore more outdoor spaces, remember that Goldendoodles are highly social and love meeting other dogs and people. However, it's important to stay engaged with your dog, even while socializing with other owners. If your dog is left to entertain themselves, they might learn to ignore you, which can make future recall training more difficult. Keep them focused on you by playing games or offering treats at intervals throughout the walk.

How Dogs Communicate and Approach Each Other

Goldendoodles are naturally curious and friendly, and they will want to greet other dogs they meet in the park. However, not all dogs will be as eager to interact, especially older dogs who may not have as much tolerance for a puppy's energy. It's important to understand how dogs communicate with each other and what signs to watch out for when they interact.

Dogs communicate through a variety of signals that show whether they are comfortable, anxious, or irritated.

Here are the key stages of dog communication to watch out for, whether it's your own dog or another dog approaching:

Early signs of discomfort

- **Yawning, looking away, licking lips, or moving away**: These are subtle signs that a dog is uncomfortable and doesn't want to engage. If you see this, it's a good idea to guide your dog away from the other dog to prevent escalating the situation.

Escalation signs:

- **Panting, hackles up, showing the whites of their eyes (whale eyes)**: This indicates that the dog is feeling threatened or anxious. This is a warning signal, and if ignored, the dog may react more strongly.

Clear warning signs:

- **Lip curling, growling, or snarling**: At this point, the dog is letting you know they are uncomfortable and may snap if provoked further.

Aggressive response:

- **Lunging or snapping**: If the earlier signals are ignored, the dog may lunge or even bite in an attempt to make the other dog or perceived threat go away.

If you notice any of these signs, calmly guide your Goldendoodle away from the situation. Pay attention to both your dog and the dogs they meet, as some may be more tolerant of puppy energy while others may not.

Body language

When dogs greet each other, body language is key. A dog running directly at another dog, face-on, is often seen as rude or even threatening. Approaching from the side is considered more polite. If your dog is running too quickly toward another dog, it's helpful to intervene early. You can distract them with a toy or call them back to you to prevent potential conflicts.

Tail position and hackles are other important signals. A tail held high and hackles raised don't always mean aggression, but they indicate high adrenaline and excitement. If you notice these signs, keep an eye on the interaction and be ready to intervene again. If a dog puts their head over another dog's shoulders, this can be a sign of dominance, and it might lead to mounting or a more serious confrontation.

Always ask the owner of another dog if it's okay for your puppy to approach, especially if their dog is on a leash. Leashed dogs can feel constrained and may react defensively if an off-leash dog runs up to them.

Encouraging Positive Interactions

To help your Goldendoodle learn proper social skills, it's important to give them positive experiences with other dogs and people. If your dog is too excited when seeing another dog, practice having them sit and stay while the other dog approaches. Reward them for staying calm and focused on you. If your dog learns that remaining calm results in praise or treats, they'll be less likely to run up to every dog they meet.

Goldendoodles are known for their friendly and playful nature, so it's important to teach them boundaries. They will naturally want to greet new dogs, but they also need to understand that not all dogs are interested in play. By managing their excitement and teaching them to approach calmly, you can prevent negative experiences and help your puppy build healthy relationships with other dogs.

Separation Anxiety

Separation training is not generally top of the training list for new puppy parents - we all know that we need to teach sit, stay, leash and potty training - but we need to add separation training to that list.

Separation Anxiety can be a form of separation distress or isolation distress - a milder form of separation anxiety. I use the terms separation anxiety as a general term but it will depend on the depth of the issue for your dog.

It happens when a dog reacts to separation (usually when their 'family' leaves the home) and this results in your dog getting stressed. This stress is released in a variety of ways, from whining and barking, to chewing and destruction, with a few poops in between.

There are a few theories on why dogs react the way that they do but the most important thing to know is that if they are suffering from any degree of separation anxiety then, for one reason or another, they are getting stressed when you leave and they are being left alone. All we need to do is to help teach them that being alone without you is not to be feared.

Dogs are not the same

Separation or canine separation anxiety can affect all dogs, although research suggests that dogs are more likely to develop separation behavioral problems if they are male, come from a shelter, or are separated from the litter before they are 60 days old.

Interestingly, dogs born at home were more likely to suffer anxiety than those born with a breeder.

Separation anxiety can, and does, occur for other reasons. It also happens to older dogs as well as with puppies.

Dogs that tend to have a high level of alertness are also thought to have an increased chance of experiencing separation anxiety but again, not all will develop separation anxiety, it just means that they can be more susceptible to it.

As we can see, separation anxiety is not specific to a particular breed but some factors might influence the likelihood of your Goldendoodle experiencing separation anxiety which is why their lineage is important.

Golden Retrievers are known for their friendly, loving, and social nature and are sometime referred to as "velcro dogs" because they love to be close to their owners and form strong attachments. This loyalty and affection makes them wonderful family pets but it can also make them more prone to separation anxiety when left alone for extended periods.

Poodles are intelligent, trainable, and versatile dogs and they too, are also affectionate but they can be more independent compared to Golden Retrievers. Known for their problem-solving abilities it is this that can help them handle being alone better than some other breeds. However, they can also develop separation anxiety if they feel neglected or isolated for long periods.

It means that very generally, if the genes of the Golden Retriever parent are the more dominant, then your Goldendoodle may inherit more of the social and attached nature of Golden Retrievers and could be more prone to separation anxiety.

Signs Of Separation Anxiety

Separation anxiety is not a failure on the owner's part. There can be many reasons that a dog reacts like this.

There may have been a change in ownership either from another home or from a shelter, there may have been a house move or a change in the routine of the family, it might be due to divorce or the loss of a family member (usually another dog but it could be a cat or even a family member moving away to school).

For puppy's, it might simply be the first time they have been left alone having been used to being around people all the time.

Dogs may also have had a bad experience - firecrackers, a delivery person, or the noise from trash pick-up. Dogs don't like sudden and unexpected noises and neither do Goldendoodles.

Like anyone, dogs can get more nervous if they are alone. But remember, dogs are not used to dealing with threats alone, they are used to packs who provide safety as well as nurture. If they are already nervous or uncomfortable then they will feel even more vulnerable when they need to deal with these 'threats' alone in their home.

Finally, dogs may be bored. Boredom usually affects young or energetic dogs who still don't know what to do when they are left to play - or relax - alone and they will seek out ways to keep themselves entertained. Like chewing furniture - this is also a calming activity - or exploring the trash. Exercise will help with this.

Dogs will do some of these things some of the time. But when they display this behavior most of the time, then it is likely your dog is suffering from some degree of separation anxiety.

When you are away

Dogs will get bored when they are left alone. Your dog will sleep – dogs sleep for between to 10 to 14 hours a day - but he will be awake at various points, and he will be looking for something to do.

He might have a sniff around, have a drink or two, and then look for something else to occupy his mind, his energy, and his time, and as we know, they like to put things in their mouth, some things fit in their mouths and some things don't. This means that sometimes the mess you discover on returning home is simply a sign of a bored dog and not necessarily one suffering from anxiety.

This doesn't make the experience of returning home any more pleasant, but exercise will help, and finding toys that he can play with will relieve some of that boredom. Other signs, that are more likely to be separation anxiety, are more obvious.

You (or your neighbour) might notice howling when you leave the house (this will usually happens almost as soon as you leave) but other signs include excessive barking, panting or whining, and indoor accidents. This won't be due to not being housebroken.

Stress can result in either peeing or pooping or both. They may also chew things to calm themselves, scratch at doors or windows and some might try to escape.

They are more likely to be scratching the door that you left from, or the window from where they can see you leave, they might chew something that smells of you - a shoe, sock, or even a magazine.

Signs of stress

Signs of general stress in dogs will be panting and pacing and this may well be evident in your dog if he is suffering from separation anxiety.

Is your dog panting when you return home? This might be due to whining and barking while you were gone. You will notice this at other times too.

Separation anxiety is not only when you leave the house and the dog is alone. It can also be when dogs become anxious when they are not seated near you or can't see you even if you are still at home.

Does your dog follow you around and want to sit beside you all the time? Does he sit against your legs or feet (this way he will know as soon as you move)?

What happens when you leave? Is it only you that your dog is focused on (if you share your home with family). In some cases, it doesn't matter if he is with another person in the home when you leave - it is specifically you that matters to him.

If you share your home and want to find this out, simply have a friend or family member stay with him (with some treats) and leave the house. How does he react? Does he ignore the treats and look for you and if he does, for how long for? Or does he settle down with the other person and enjoy his treats?

If you are not sure how your dog is reacting when you leave then it is useful to record your dog when you are not there. What does he do when you leave? Does he go to the door for a few minutes - how long? Take note of everything you can see and what he does. This is one of the best ways to find out what is happening when you are gone.

Signs of anxiety

Does your dog start to behave differently as you get ready to leave, before you have started to get ready or when you are getting ready to leave? Some dogs react to the picking up of a coat or keys. They might start pacing, panting or look plain miserable when you start to do this, or if you pack a bag or a case.

The first thing to do is to take note of their behavior and try and think about whether it has changed and why it might have changed. What changes have you made, if any?

Notice how much and how often your dog is following you (even if he is a new puppy). If it's an older dog try to think back to any changes - is he sitting beside you more often, following your more than he used to? Is there any other reason or a point in time that you can identify?

The solution to this part of their behavior is to slowly build them up to being comfortable with you not being beside or near them so that they get used to your absence and learn (or re-learn) that you come back.

It is perfectly natural for dogs to show some anxiety - so don't over-react or worry about it. But if they do suffer from anxiety or nervousness, it is more likely they will also suffer from separation anxiety.

Sometimes any or some of the signs can be displayed for other reasons, so if you are worried at all just check with your veterinarian.

Preparation

It's a good idea to get your puppy used to being separated from you when they are young. Even if you don't expect to be away from them often, there will be times when you will need to be.

Teaching your puppy not to fear this absence, and to let them know that they can be relaxed when you are not there, is one of the best things you can do for both your puppy, and for yourself.

If your puppy can get used to being left for short periods when he is young, then he is more likely to grow up feeling relaxed and comfortable when he is left on his own for a period of time or part of the day.

Get him used to not being beside you

These are all really simple things to do and are obvious once you know them. You will need to do this slowly, teaching them bit by bit over time.

The first 4 basic steps that you need to take are the following ones.

1. Pick the room you want your puppy or dog to be in when you are not in the house. Decide which room this is going to be as early as you can.

2. Once you decide on the location, start getting them used to being in this room - don't wait until the time when you are going to leave the house. Make sure you have left their basked, bed or crate in the same room

3. Spend time with your puppy in this room - you want them to understand it is not a punishment 'place' or a place that is apart from you, but a part of their household. For example if it is the kitchen and his crate is in the kitchen, have him go into the crate while you are also in the kitchen or create an area that you can block off (and have his crate in).

4. Once you have picked the room that you want your puppy to stay in when you leave the house, create a gate to the room or area by making a barrier so that your puppy can still see you. Again, for example, if the crate is in the kitchen, close the door but remain in the kitchen having a coffee or cooking or just reading. As long as he can see you. Remember not to interact with your puppy when he is there - just go about doing things as normal.

If you have a kitchen counter or an island that has a space under it, put the crate there. I saw someone do this recently and their puppy was happy wandering in and out of their crate, or lying happily sleeping as the rest of the household milled around the room. Their crate really was the puppy's happy, safe place.

You are aiming to spend time in this room when you are **not** about to leave, so make sure that you spend time there during the day, or when you are training them, so that this becomes a place that you are a part of too. You want being in this room and apart from you as a part of their normal day ie. there is no stress for them in not being beside you all the time.

To achieve this you need to start the next stage of their training.

Initially you are going to close the gate but remain beside it. Do this for 2 or 3 minutes but, if your dog starts to get stressed, just calmly open it again.

Keep building their confidence and slowly make the time longer. Start moving around and doing other things as you build up the time and distance. At this point, you will always be in sight.

If they start to get anxious just move forward or return to the point when they were comfortable. Once they are comfortable with the distance, start to move out of sight for a few minutes, and then repeat the process of stretching the time.

Then move into another room out of sight (but they will still be able to hear and smell you). Return after a few minutes, and then repeat building up the time as you go along.

Finally, go to the main door and go outside for a few minutes. Once again, repeat the process of increasing the time you are away and check how your dog is reacting.

If you notice any signs of stress or anxiety then go back a couple of steps and begin building up your dog's confidence once again.

Keep the time as short as you need to, it can start with as little as 5 or 10 seconds, and build the time based on your dog's response.

From the very start let the dog know that the place you have chosen is their safe place. Keep all their things in this room and place their bed or crate in here as soon as you can, along with some toys and chews.

If you are using a crate, keep the crate door open - let them get used to going in and out of the crate and choosing to do so.

Get some chew toys for them. Chew toys are good because chewing is calming action (and it's why they chew things they shouldn't). You could also put an item of your clothing in the room so that they can more easily smell you and feel more secure.

A Kong is a great chew toy to use because, as well as the chewing, the fun of getting the treats or food out of the inside of the Kong exercises their mind. Giving your dog a reason to exercise his mind keeps him happily occupied.

Put on some sound - like a radio talk station. Not at a high volume - you only want to muffle any unexpected sounds. Your dog will be paying attention to any noise they hear, so this can help disguise some of the day-to-day noises that might go on outside (or inside) your home. It is useful to do this as soon as you begin the training to get them used to it.

Try to teach your dog not to follow you all the time in the home. You want him to feel comfortable being in a separate room from you. Don't force this or make him feel stressed about it. You can do this by playing the following game (but you won't be able to do this until you have taught him the 'stay' cue).

Ask him to remain in one room while you move to another, then come back. If he stays where he was, when you come back, give him a reward. Remember, when you come back not to increase or cause excitement, you want to keep him calm. Once again, extend the time that you are not in the room while he 'stays'. This can be a great game for your dog and he will enjoy it as much as you enjoy the results of it.

When you are ready to start the next phase of actually leaving the house there are a few more things you can do to keep your dog calm while you are out.

Leaving and returning

Start by leaving the house for a minute, 2 minutes, 3 minutes, and so on, and try and return before they are anxious. If you notice they are not comfortable, then go back to the point when they were, and start from there again to gradually build the time.

Aim to build the routine - perhaps a treat as you leave. But don't kiss and cuddle them and make a fuss with gestures and by your comments. Try and make it as normal and calm as possible. This is incredibly important and remarkably effective. Just remember, never make a fuss of your dog when you are leaving are returning.

Once you start leaving altogether, do so for short periods at the start if you can, and build up the time to 2, 3 and 4 hours. Do everything as normal - and make sure they have something to play with.

You might start to notice that your dog starts to get anxious when you put on your shoes or coat or if you pick up keys or a bag.

If they start to react to these signs then start training them to get used to these things. Put on your shoes or coat or grab your keys but don't leave. Do something else or sit down and relax (or watch the TV). Keep doing this during the day so that they don't associate these actions with your departure.

Take this slowly - leave and come back. Build their knowledge and confidence. Having them exercised will help reduce their energy levels so remember to make sure they have had a walk and have been fed. You can also try giving them a favorite treat. This might help them associate your departure with something they can look forward to.

You might need to go back a few paces in the separation training from time-to-time, as you are building their confidence and their sense of 'normal'.

Remember, if they have done something wrong on your return don't punish them or shout at them. They won't understand why.

Summary

- Don't make a fuss of your dog when you leave. Don't kiss them and say 'goodbye'.
- Leave calmly.
- Give them their favorite treat as you leave - give them something to chew on.
- Make sure they have been exercised.
- Don't excite them as soon as you return home, wait a few minutes before greeting them.

Leaving when using a crate

When you put your dog in their crate (if you use a crate) before you leave then don't close the door right away. Put them in and wait until they calm down or lie down.

This might take a few minutes or more so do something else and give them time to relax and be calm. Close and open the door a few times if you like, but wait until they lie down before you close the door.

Don't bribe them into the crate with a treat and then immediately shut the door - just take your time, and let them take their time to get

Once they are comfortable in their space and their room then you can start moving away using the methods detailed in the first step.

Punishment Won't Work

Before we talk about all the things that can be done to help with separation anxiety, it is useful to understand why punishment just won't work.

Have you ever taken your dog over to the 'scene of the crime' and pointed at it? Did you notice that the dog appears to 'look guilty' and maybe cowered. We, as humans, project our own interpretation onto this behavior, and assume that the dog is noticing what it has done and feels 'guilty' about it.

This is not what is happening.

What we see as 'looking guilty' is appeasement behavior. It can be a way that your dog is releasing tension to try and get rid of their fear. The cowering, flat ears and tail between the legs, or looking away, is your dog trying to placate you.

Your dog might know that he has emptied the trash all over the kitchen floor and that he dragged it around the house (and that it was fun), but he won't connect what he has done minutes or hours later to why you are behaving the way that you are towards him right now.

All your dog will know is that you are not happy with him and he will be fearful, and although he will try to placate you, he won't know what he has done. No matter how much you point at that mess your dog is not going to know why you are angry with him - and that anger will scare him.

The worst part is that it means that administering 'punishment' or anger when you return home and have encountered a mess will make your dog stressed about you coming home. He will already have been stressed about you leaving, and he will have been stressed while you were away. Punishment when you return home can make any anxiety worse.

Just remember, your dog has not done this to deliberately annoy you nor to 'get back' at you. Dogs just don't think like that. They did it because they were stressed and anxious or bored and they tried to use that pent-up energy.

They might look 'guilty' when you return because they have learned that they got into trouble the last time you came home - so they appease you as soon as you return to prevent it as much as they can.

Health and Wellbeing

The most important aspect to remember here is that Goldendoodles are generally very healthy - and this is because breeders have tried their best to 'breed out' many of the most common problems that many breeds encounter. But, it's always worth being familiar with some of the problems that you may hear about from time-to-time as well as the more general health practices that you might come across (and those you will need to know about).

Hybrid Vigor

Hybrid Vigor will be a term that you hear when you are talking to breeders about your Goldendoodle. It is particular to dogs that are from different breeds and, essentially, it's all about 'strengthening' the DNA.

The genes in DNA include alleles, and these alleles can contain disorders and diseases, but they need two to tango - one from the mother and one from the father.

Essentially, an allele will not express itself if there is only one copy of that allele in a gene. It means that it won't be 'active' and affect the health of your dog if there is only one copy rather than two.

Purebred dogs come from a narrow gene pool of DNA - and certainly a narrower gene pool than that of a hybrid dog like your Goldendoodle. The theory goes that this means there is a higher chance of both the mother and the father carrying an allele, and therefore a higher chance of purebred dogs passing down unwanted alleles to their puppies.

Which brings us back to our Goldendoodle. Hybrids, in effect, provide the opportunity to widen the gene pool that provides more 'good' allele options to choose from.

This is what the breeder aims to do when they are selecting the parents - they are aiming to 'iron-out' any historic disorders or diseases from each breed line.

The Animal Health Trust explained this in a press release, "Because of the small gene pool in purebred dogs, inherited diseases resulting from single gene mutations are more likely to occur than in their cross bred cousins".

It all means that, if both parents suffer from the same condition, the pups could be affected. Likewise, if both parents don't suffer from the condition, or only one parent does, then the resulting puppies won't be affected.

Here's where it gets complicated. If one of the resulting puppies carries the allele from the one parent who as it in their gene, and they are later bred with with another dog that has this same single allele, it can create 2 of them in their puppies i.e. the net generation.

It all means that hybrid dogs, on average, should be healthier than the purebred breed from which they came, but just being a cross-breed is no guarantee of better health.

If your Goldendoodle breeder claims that there is no need to do any health checks because the puppies benefit from hybrid vigor, it isn't true.

Testing and Common Conditions

The Goldendoodle is not recognized as a standard breed by major kennel clubs like the American Kennel Club (AKC) or the Kennel Club (UK).

Since Goldendoodles are a mixed breed resulting from crossing a Golden Retriever and a Poodle, they do not have a dedicated National Breed Club that sets specific breeding guidelines or recommended tests but, as with any mixed breed, we can look at the parent breeds.

For information and to guide you, should you be concerned about any problems in the future, we cover some of the problems that can be specific to the parent breeds of the Poodle and Golden Retriever.

Don't worry too much because, overall, like their parent breeds, Goldendoodles don't have many, or any, major health issues.

The National Breed Club recommend the following tests:

Poodles

The Poodle Club of America (PCA) is the national breed club for Poodles in the United States. The PCA recommends the following health tests for Poodles:

- **Hip and Elbow Evaluation:** Similar to Golden Retrievers, Poodles should undergo hip evaluations through methods such as the Orthopedic Foundation for Animals (OFA) hip evaluation. This helps detect hip dysplasia, a hereditary condition that affects the hip joints.
- **Eye Examination:** Regular eye exams by a veterinary ophthalmologist are essential to identify and prevent hereditary eye diseases that can affect Poodles, such as progressive retinal atrophy (PRA) and cataracts.
- **Optigen PRA Testing:** This is a specific genetic test for progressive retinal atrophy (PRA), a group of inherited eye diseases that can lead to blindness in Poodles.
- **von Willebrand's Disease (vWD) Testing:** vWD is a genetic bleeding disorder that can affect some Poodles. Genetic testing can identify carriers and ensure responsible breeding practices.
- **Cardiac Evaluation:** Cardiac testing helps assess the heart health of Poodles and can detect potential heart issues.

- **Sebaceous Adenitis (SA) Testing:** Sebaceous adenitis is a skin disorder that can affect some Poodles, and genetic testing can identify carriers of this condition.

Generally speaking Poodles are in good health.They will suffer from a range of minor problems, as most dogs do. Eye, knee, and hip tests are advised, as are DNA tests, which can identify PRA and von Willebrand's Disease.

Golden Retrievers

The Golden Retriever Club of America (GRCA) is the national breed club for Golden Retrievers in the United States. The American Kennel Club and the GRCA recommend the first 5 tests, while GRCA add an additional test - the ETT.

- **Hip Evaluation:** The most common method is the Orthopedic Foundation for Animals (OFA) hip evaluation, which involves X-rays to check for hip dysplasia. Good hip health is essential to ensure the dog's mobility and comfort.
- **Elbow Evaluation:** Similar to the hip evaluation, the OFA also conducts elbow evaluations to check for elbow dysplasia, another hereditary condition that affects joint health.
- **Eye Examination:** Like Poodles, regular eye exams by a veterinary ophthalmologist can identify and prevent hereditary eye diseases such as progressive retinal atrophy (PRA) and cataracts.
- **Heart Evaluation:** Golden Retrievers may be prone to certain heart conditions, and a cardiac evaluation can help detect any issues early on.

- **Genetic Testing:** Genetic tests can identify carriers of specific hereditary diseases, such as progressive retinal atrophy (PRA1 and PRA2), muscular dystrophy (MD), and Neuronal Ceroid Lipofuscinosis 5 (Golden Retriever) (NCL, NCL5).
- **Exercise Tolerance Test (ETT):** The ETT tests the dog's ability to handle physical activity and assesses its cardiac health during exercise (this test is recommended by the GRCA and not the Kennel Club)

Elbow and Hip Dysplasia

Poodles can be prone to hip and elbow dysplasia that usually progresses with age but it may start to be visible when still a puppy. It is an inherited disease, and is caused when the ball and sockets of the joint bones don't 'fit' properly and have a tendency to slip out. Screening of parent dogs is actively encouraged so that only dogs with sound joints are used for breeding.

It causes the joint to form abnormally which can cause not only pain but mobility problems. Early signs can be a wobbly walk or your puppy lying with splayed back legs (best described as looking like a frog). If your puppy does this it might be nothing to do with dysplasia but if you are worried you can ask your veterinarian to test his for the disease. There are a number of treatments including medication, physiotherapy and even surgery.

In the long term, that constant inflammation can lead to joint remodeling and premature arthritis. For some dogs, this can be disabling and impair their enjoyment of life, which is all the more heartbreaking because this can happen to young dogs.

Management of hip or elbow dysplasia means being careful of the puppy's activity levels whilst his bones are still maturing.

In addition, giving a joint supplement can help to protect the joint surfaces.

Dogs with mild dysplasia can often be managed with rest and pain-relieving medications, however, those most seriously affected may need surgery, including specialist replacement joint surgery.

The best way to ensure your dog is less prone to any of these conditions is to buy from a reputable breeder and to ensure you get health clearances from both of the parents.

Luxating Patella

This is more common in Toy Poodles than Standard Poodles.

A Luxating Patella is fairly common in dogs and is is where the kneecap (patella) shifts sideways at the front of the knee. It can also be know as a dislocated kneecap.

The main symptom that is not often seen with other conditions is the sudden lifting of one hind limb. I have a dog with this condition. He lifts his leg for no apparent reason off the ground for a short time and continues to try and play. Some dogs will yelp when this happens while others, like my own dog, shows no signs of pain or discomfort. This is sometimes called a "skip" by both owners and vets.

Depending on the eternity of the condition rest or complete rest might be recommended. If it is severe then there is an operation that can might help but as with any surgery, that too, comes with risks and complications.

Osteohondrodysplasia

Osteochondrodysplasia is a disorder ("dysplasia") of bones (" osteo") and cartilage ("chondro"). It is an inherited condition and that needs a mutated gene from each parent.

It was discovered in the Miniature Poodle in Britain in 1956 when it was first described a crippling dwarfism. It is a form of skeletal dysplasia that stunts growth and impairs movement and it can be seen when a pup is only 3 weeks old. Affected pups soon exhibit abducted hind limbs, enlarged joints, flattening of the rib cage, shortened and bent long bones, undershot jaws, and elongated and misshapen paws that resemble clubfoot.

Affected dogs can survive for many years with supportive care and they will develop arthritis and might have breathing difficulty due to their deformed ribcages.

It is not known how rare or common this is but it can be tested for and is one of the reason you need to ensure that you know the test for both of your puppy's parents. This is important if you intend your puppy to have a litter because a dog can be a carrier without any symptoms.

Gastric Dilatation Volvulus (GDV) or Bloat

Poodle's can be prone to something called Gastric Dilatation Volvulus (GDV). This is when the stomach fills with air and twists on its axis preventing the passage of food and water which can stop the flow of circulation to the stomach and intestines. This can be life-threatening.

It is a serious condition and as soon as this happens you must take your dog to the vet right away. If the stomach is not returned to its natural position then it can be fatal.

To prevent this happening, try not to feed him for at least 30-45 minutes before exercise and don't feed him until as least 30-45 minutes after exercise. You can also reduce the chances of bloat by feeding small meals spread throughout the day and by using a bowl designed to make it difficult for your dog to eat too quickly.

Von Willebrand Disease - this is a blood clotting disorder frequently found in Toy and Miniature Poodles. Ask your breeder for the test - this is a DNA test.

Ears and Skin

You should clean your pups ears regularly to prevent earwax from accumulating and to reduce the chance of infection.

If you notice a smell, or you notice black or brown wax, or his ear looks red and he is scratching it then he may have an ear infection.

Otitis Externa is one of the most common conditions amongst many dog breeds but is more likely to affect Cocker Spaniels, Poodles, Bassets and GSD's - you will notice a wax build-up or a smell and probably both.

Otitis is also often one of the illnesses that insurance companies exclude from policies as an on-going condition so check this out before you enrol. This is probably due to the fact that, once susceptible, it is likely to keep recurring.

Regularly cleaning his ears can make all the difference to preventing Otitis taking hold - but don't over-clean as this can actually make it worse. This is one of those times where it's helpful to talk to your veterinarian.

Ask about appropriate ear care products and if you are worried about how to clean his ears, then just ask your veterinarian to show you how best to clean them.

To get him used to having his ears touched make sure you remember to touch and caress them when he is a puppy.

Like the ears, allergies can cause problems with the skin and they can lead to *dermatitis* (skin inflammation). They can be caused by many things including pollen or dust mites, items your dog eats (for example, wheat), items that your dog comes into contact with (for example, washing powders), or bites from parasites such as fleas.

As allergies cannot be cured, treatment might be needed for the rest of his life. But it is usually very effective and won't impact him other than requiring regular medication, and there are some herbal options available and diet can help too, so don't forget to ask about these.

Sebaceous Adenitis

Sebaceous adenitis is a rare inflammatory skin disease that affects the skin glands of young and middle age dogs. It tends to effect the Standard Poodle. Symptoms include Alopecia, mild scaling of skin along the head, trunk and ears and there might be a secondary bacterial infection along the hairline (more common in long haired breeds).

The cause is still unknown and if your dog is diagnosed with this then you might want to be included in a tracking survey so that more can be found out about this disease.

Eyes

Progressive retinal atrophy (PRA)

PRA this tends to effect the Miniature Poodle and it is a part of the test that your breeder will carry out.

The retina is part of the central nervous system. In retinal degeneration, the cells of the retina stop working leading to impaired vision and blindness. There are lots of causes for retinal degeneration including other eye conditions, diet, reactions to other drugs, genetics.

Providing your dog with a balanced diet (that includes meat), a low-fat diet could also help improve or slow the degeneration.

Glaucoma

Also ask your breeder if the Poodles parents have been recently screened for Glaucoma. Poodles suffer from Glaucoma (Toy Poodles appear to be most prone to this). Symptoms include squinting, watery eyes, bluing of the cornea, and redness in the whites of the eyes and it is very painful.

Eyelash disorders

Trichiasis, distichiasis, and ectopic cilia are eyelash conditions that are more common in Miniature and Toy Poodles and some other dog breeds.

Whether causes by an in-growing eyelash (Trichiasis) or ones that grow from inside the eyelid (ectopic cilia) all of them can damage the cornea of the eye and can also cause conjunctivitis. In all cases you will notice and overflow of tears.

Teeth

You will start getting your puppy used to having something in his mouth at an early age so that he will be comfortable with you cleaning his teeth when he gets older and needs it.

Use a dog tooth brush or, if you don't have one, then you can use a child's toothbrush. You should clean his teeth at last twice a week, and ideally every day. You can also use a dog dental chew. They love these, just don't overdo it - remember they are not treats.

Nails

Trim his nails once or twice a month. If you tend to walk on hard surfaces his nails will get worn down naturally and you may only need to get his nails checked or cut when he goes to the groomer. If you can hear them clicking on the floor, they might be too long.

Dog toenails have blood vessels in them, and if you cut too far you can cause bleeding so you might want to start by watching a groomer or asking for help from your veterinarian.

Dew claws

The first thing to point out is that dogs very rarely have dew claws in their hind legs - they are almost always only seen in the front legs - just above their pad and below the carpal pad. I tend to think about it as a thumb because it really is a thumb. While you can expect your pup to have two dewclaws, this is not the case for all breeds. The Great Pyrenees, for example, should have six dewclaws, one on each front leg and two on each hind leg and this is an AKC requirement.

Dew claws used to be removed from puppies when they were very young (anywhere between two and five days old) to 'conform to the breed standard'.

The practice of automatically removing dew claws in very young puppies is not as common these days. One of the reasons is that dew claws are attached to other tendons and muscles.

The front dew claws contain two bones. Attached to these bones are four tendons and two muscles. Once the dew claw is removed, these muscles are then left to atrophy, weakening the entire structure of the carpus and this can cause arthritis.

The dew claws function is to stabilize the carpal joint when the dog is running or when he is making sharp turns. This stabilizing action gives additional traction and reduces the tension on the front leg. If a dog does not have its front dew claws, the leg will twist on its axis to overcompensate. This increases the pressure on the carpus and in turn, the rest of the forelimb all the way up to the shoulder.

A study published by the Journal of the American Veterinary Medical Association in 2018 looked at the risk factors for injuries in dogs involved with agility events. They concluded that the absence of the front dewclaws was one of the greatest factors "associated with significantly increased odds of injury".

Loss of Blood/Weight

One of the first questions you should get asked by a veterinarian if you need to make an emergency call because your dog has had an injury is "is your dog bleeding". The reason they ask this is not because a dog can lose a lot of blood but that, even a small loss of blood, can be dangerous. Just two teaspoons per pound of weight can be enough to put your dog into shock. It is for this reason, if nothing else, that it is useful to always know the weight of your dog.

Eating poop

It is not uncommon for a puppy to eat his poop - around 25% of them do it. Sometimes it is something they copied from watching their mother. When puppies are very young, and before they are weaned a mother eats her puppy's poop. This can continue during the early part of weaning. For us humans, it's quite hard to watch but it's perfectly natural for dogs. It is thought that it dates back to the days when they lived in the wild when the mother would need to keep the den clean and free from poop to protect the den from predators (and infections). For some puppies they will watch and learn this behavior but it usually doesn't last long.

Sometimes it's simply because puppies love taste and textures, and poop has both of these, plus it carries lots of interesting scents that has lots of information. Who the owner might be, what did they eat? And don't forget, puppies only have their mouths to explore with.

Research has found that dogs most likely to eat poop are hungry. If he is continuing to eat poop then make sure that you are feeding his at the correct intervals, and in the correct amounts and prefer-ably to a schedule. You might also want to check that the food contains enough of the ingredients that he needs.

They can also eat poop because they are bored or stressed. Make sure he is not being left alone for too long and is getting plenty of stimulation. If you need to work, and are out of the house, try and get a dog sitter to visit.

Of all the reasons your puppy is eating poop the least likely is a nutritional deficiency in his diet. If he suddenly starts eating poop, especially if he is a bit older, then it might be due to a medical problem and in this instance you should contact your veterinarian.

To Spay or to Neuter your dog ?

Every dog owner is going to come up against this question but there really isn't any definitive right or wrong answer, either on the best timing or whether it needs to be done at all.

In the USA vets tend to recommend that pups are neutered or spayed as early as possible, usually around 8 weeks. In Europe and the UK most vets recommend 6–9 months and some recommend waiting until 10-24 months for males while females should be allowed to have at least two seasons.

It is now generally recommended that your dog has reached maturity before being spayed or neutered. This is because neutering and spaying removes hormones from your dog which have an important role to play in their development. These hormones regulate growth, mood, muscle, bone growth and density.

Some studies have shown an increased rate of, for example, Hip Dysplasia, in dogs that have been neutered before maturity. If there is no medical reason to do it early, waiting until your dog reaches maturity might be better.

If you are in ay doubt then ask your veterinarian.

Overheating

High internal temperatures can be a serious health issue for all dogs. It can lead to organ failure and even death. Dog's don't sweat - they can only do so via their paws and they cool themselves by panting.

A dog's internal temperature is normally around 100 to 102.5, and a temperature of 105 or above is considered to be a crisis.

The most common culprit of critical overheating is the car. Cars can heat up very, very fast. A car parked in the sun can reach a temperature of 116 within 60 minutes. The interior, such as the dashboard, can even reach over 150 degrees Farenheit.

- Cracking a window won't help much - but if you have a sunroof or moon roof then leave that open at all times. Heat rises and so this will help but it won't remove the problem.

If you already know about the car then you now need to think about your walk and exercise - especially if it there are high temperatures and high humidity.

- Try to avoid walking your dog on hot pavements especially asphalt. Black asphalt not only retains heat but it radiates heat. Your dog will be much closer to this heat than you are.

- If you dog has been playing he might not think about having a drink. Make sure he has a good drink before your walk and afterwards.

- If your dog is panting heavily and his tongue is hanging out and you notice he is more lethargic or slower than normal then your dog might be overheating. You need to get him out of the sun and cool him down right away.

- One of the best ways to cool him down is to get him into cool water. The best heat transfer points are paws, groin, and cheeks so if for any reason you can't get him into a bath or a natural water source then put cool water over these areas first - along with his tummy.

- Shaving off all of his coat is not believed to work very well (and can actually aide the heating process because his coat actually protects him from the heat too) but shaving his tummy can be a good idea and helps you cover his groin area faster.

And now we move on to finding a breeder - be sure to check any of the health issues mentioned in this chapter.

How to find a breeder

Responsible breeders focus on producing healthy puppies with good temperaments, proper socialization, and suitable conformation to ensure they are well-suited for their future homes. They prioritize the overall health and well-being of their breeding dogs and make efforts to minimize the risk of passing on genetic health issues to their puppies.

Reputable - or ethical - breeders invest in good quality dog food, they have good veterinary care, they tend to only breed their females up to twice year and they work to established breeding plans. All of this means that they spend more on the care of the dogs which is why the cost will be higher. If you find a breeder and they offer you a low price then you can be pretty sure they are not reputable.

You should expect to be asked questions about the puppy's care and you may be asked to sign a contract that deals with health and should include a return to breeder clause that means you will return the puppy if you can no longer care for him or her.

If you are not quizzed about how you will care for your puppy then it is likely, no matter how high the cost, that you are not dealing with a reputable breeder.

Other things that can help identify a reputable breeder will be if they have extensive knowledge of their breed and the generations. They will ideally work with a vet, undertake health screening, and if you have been on a wait list, this is another good sign.

They should also be able to show genetic screening and the lineage of your puppy (which should be extensive).

How to recognise a puppy farm

When you are buying a puppy, you might not recognise that you're buying from a puppy farm. Many of these types of sellers are experienced and go to extremes to cover up what they really are.

A puppy farm isn't always obvious, so look out for some important signs at each stage of purchasing your puppy.

Advertising

If you see an advert online, check how many other adverts that the seller is running. A puppy farm is more than likely to be advertising more than one litter and may also be advertising different breeds. To check, you can google the number in the advert to find out how often it is being used and for what.

If the advert claims the puppy has been vaccinated and the puppy is under 6 weeks old then this would indicate the advert is from a puppy farm. (Always request written evidence that your puppy and his mother, and if required, both parents, have been vaccinated).

If your puppy comes with a passport (and has been imported), make sure that your puppy is 12 weeks old. They should be this age to qualify for a passport. If there is no passport then it is more likely your puppy has come from a country with poor legislation around puppy farming.

Always make sure that you see the puppy at his home and where he has been born.

Make sure that you see the mum and note how the mother reacts to the seller as well as the overall condition of the mum. She should not be wary of the breeder. But also note how she reacts to the puppy. You want to be sure that she is the mother and not another dog that is being presented to you as the mum.

As noted above, the breeder should be asking you lots of questions to make sure you can look after your new puppy. If they are not interested in you and how you will care for the puppy, then they are unlikely to be interested in the puppy's welfare.

Puppy farms often prefer to deal with cash and do not offer refunds or have a no returns policy. You should always seek a puppy contract that lays out the responsibilities and a returns policy.

Health Clearances

A good breeder will show you health clearances for both of your puppy's parents. Health clearances prove that a dog has been tested for, and cleared for, a particular condition. While there might not be a specific National Breed Club for Goldendoodles, reputable breeders typically follow guidelines and recommendations similar to those established by recognized breed clubs for the parent breeds (Golden Retrievers and Poodles).

For example, for both Golden Retrievers and Poodles, health testing may include:

Hip and Elbow Evaluations: X-rays to check for hip dysplasia and elbow dysplasia, both of which can be hereditary conditions.

Eye Examinations: To screen for common eye disorders such as progressive retinal atrophy (PRA) and cataracts.

Genetic Testing: To identify carriers of certain hereditary diseases and avoid breeding dogs that may pass on these conditions to their offspring.

Cardiac Evaluations: Some breeds, including Golden Retrievers and Poodles, may be susceptible to certain heart conditions, and cardiac evaluations can help identify potential issues.

Other Health Assessments: Depending on the breed's known health issues, breeders may also conduct tests for conditions such as von Willebrand's disease or thyroid disorders.

Health clearances are not issued to dogs younger than 2 years of age. That's because some health problems don't appear until a dog reaches full maturity. For this reason, it's often recommended that dogs not be bred until they are two or three years old.

Conclusion

It is hard to describe what a rewarding and lovable dog the Goldendoodle is., nor how much they will love you!

Just remember that they want to please you and that they will watch and learn from what you do and what you say in order to do this.

We used to train dogs by breaking their spirit. I know for sure that if you love a dog, you can't break it's spirit if you train it properly, and in partnership with him.

Dog training is not about control nor dominance - it is only about finding a language so that we can each provide the love and the life that we both want for each other.

That is what dog training is all about. It is just trying to communicate in a language that can never be a verbal two-way communication. We will never really talk to our dogs. And yet, we do.

Take the time, and learn as much from your Goldendoodle as you think they are learning from you.

Don't ever be mistaken - they are training us too!

Need more help?

I tested this and free online workshop on training your dog to become as well-behaved as a service dog. I loved it and I have decided to add it to end of my book.

The workshop is designed to help "normal" dogs like yours have the same level of calmness, obedience and impulse control as service dogs.

It's being conducted by Dr. Alexa Diaz (one of the top service dog trainers in the U.S.) and Eric Presnall (host of the hit Animal Planet TV show "Who Let the Dogs Out").

The techniques described in the workshop are fairly groundbreaking, and ones that I love - I haven't seen many people talk of these techniques.

This is because it's the first time ever (at least that I know of) that anyone has revealed the techniques used by the service dog training industry to train service dogs.

And more importantly, how any "regular" dog owner can apply the same techniques to train their own dogs to become as well-trained.

It's not a live workshop - it's a pre-recorded workshop, which means that you can watch it at any time.

However, while the workshop is free, I am not sure whether it's going to be online for too long, so please check it out as soon as you can.

Here is the link if you are reading on kindle.

Or you can use this QR code if you have the paperback.

Resources and Citations

E. (2015, May 1). *Dogs of Durer*. The Hidden Secrets in Albrecht Durer's Art and Life. http://www.albrechtdurerblog.com/the-dogs-of-durer/

Churchill, K. W. (2022, April). The Great Ones. *The Canine Chronicles*, 150–160. http://www.onlinedigitalpubs.com/publication/?m=2330&i=743244&p=170&id=8717&ver=html5

Braaksma, H. (2022, March 4). *Poodle (Standard)*. Daily Paws. https://www.dailypaws.com/dogs-puppies/dog-breeds/standard-poodle

Alt, K. (2020, August 14). *Am I Ready For A Dog? How To Be A Responsible Dog Owner*. Canine Journal. https://www.canine-journal.com/am-i-ready-for-a-dog

Animal Poison Control. (n.d.). The American Society for the Prevention of Cruelty to Animals® (ASPCA®). https://www.aspca.org/pet-care/animal-poison-control/people-foods-avoid-feeding-your-pets

Answer These 5 Questions to Find the Right Dog For You. (2017, November 2). American Kennel Club. https://www.akc.org/expert-advice/lifestyle/answer-5-questions-find-right-dog/

Blue Cross For Pets. (n.d.). Blue Cross For Pets. https://www.bluecross.org.uk/advice/dog

SpiritDog Training. (2021, July 14). *Poodle Colors: 12 Amazing Color Variations From Common To Rare.* https://spiritdogtraining.com/breeds/poodle-colors/

Committee on Nutrient Requirements of Dogs and Cats. (2006). *Your Dog's Nutritional Needs. Retrieved.* (2006). Https://Www.Nap.Edu. https://www.nap.edu/resource/10668/dog_nutrition_final_fix.pdf

Poodles » JaneDogs. (n.d.). Jane Dogs. https://janedogs.com/poodles/

What Size Dog Crate Do You Need? (n.d.). Cooper's Crates (www.Cooperscrates.Com). https://cooperscrates.com/pages/selecting-the-correct-kennel-size

Poodle Puppy Teething and Chewing Problems for All Ages. (n.d.-b). All Poodle Info. http://www.allpoodleinfo.com/poodle-teething-chewing

Your Complete Guide to First-Year Puppy Vaccinations. (2021, February 5). American Kennel Club (Www.Akc.Org). https://www.akc.org/expert-advice/health/puppy-shots-complete-guide

Gibeault, MSc, CPDT, S. (2021, February 3). *How To Teach Your Dog To Sit.* Https://Www.Akc.Org/. https://www.akc.org/expert-advice/training/how-to-teach-your-dog-to-sit/

Madson, MA, CBCC-KA, CPDT-KA, C. (2020, July 25). *How To Teach Your Dog To Come When Called*. Https://Www.Preventivevet.Com/. https://www.preventivevet.com/dogs/how-to-teach-your-dog-to-come-when-called

PetMD Editorial. (2017, April 14). *Inflammatory Skin Disease in Dogs*. PetMD. https://www.petmd.com/dog/conditions/skin/c_dg_sebaceous_adenitis

Recall Training. (n.d.). Https://Www.Doglistener.Co.Uk. https://www.doglistener.co.uk/behavioural/recall_training.shtml

Simply Behaviour. (n.d.). *Simply Behaviour*. Http://Www.Simplybehaviour.Com/. http://www.simplybehaviour.com/

Yin, D. S. (n.d.). *Teaching Rover To Race To You In Cue*. Cattledog Publishing. https://drsophiayin.com/blog/entry/teaching_rover_-to_race_to_you_on_cue/

https://www.thelabradorsite.com/teaching-a-dog-to-heel/

Salonen, M., Sulkama, S., Mikkola, S. *et al. Prevalence, comorbidity, and breed differences in canine anxiety in 13,700 Finnish pet dogs. Sci Rep* **10,** 2962 (2020).https://doi.org/10.1038/s41598-020-59837-z

Barbara L. Sherman, Daniel S. Mills, *Canine Anxieties and Phobias: An Update on Separation Anxiety and Noise Aversions, Veterinary Clinics of North America*: Small Animal Practice, Volume 38, Issue 5, 2008, Pages 1081-1106, ISSN 0195-5616, https://doi.org/10.1016/j.cvsm.2008.04.012

Blue Cross For Pets, Retrieved from https://www.bluecross.org.uk/pet-advice/home-alone-separation-anxiety-dogs

Tiira, Katriina & Lohi, Hannes. (2015). *Early Life Experiences and Exercise Associate with Canine Anxieties. PloS one.* 10. e0141907. 10.1371/journal.pone.0141907. Retrieved from https://www.researchgate.net/publication/283492761_Early_Life_Experiences_and_Exercise_Associate_with_Canine_Anxieties

Dog Psychology 101, https://dogpsychology101.com/

Pet Poison helpline https://www.petpoisonhelpline.com/pet-owners/emergency/

Debra C. Sellon, Katherine Martucci, John R. Wenz, Denis J. Marcellin-Little, Michelle Powers, Kimberley L. Cullen. A survey of risk factors for digit injuries among dogs training and competing in agility events. J Am Vet Med Assoc 2018;252:75-83

The Kennel Club. (n.d.). *Why does my dog eat poop.* Https://Www.Thekennelclub.Org.Uk. https://www.thekennelclub.org.uk/health-and-dog-care/health/health-and-care/a-z-of-health-and-care-issues/why-does-my-dog-eat-poop/

dogtime.com/dog-breeds/cockapoo. (n.d.). Dogtime.Com. https://dogtime.com/dog-breeds/cockapoo#/slide/1

Debra C. Sellon, Katherine Martucci, John R. Wenz, Denis J. Marcellin-Little, Michelle Powers, Kimberley L. Cullen. (2018). A survey of risk factors for digit injuries among dogs training and competing in agility events. *PubMed: J Am Vet Med Association.* https://doi.org/10.2460/javma.252.1.75

Dew claws. (n.d.). Mill Creek Family Farms. https://www.millcreekfamilyfarms.com/dew-claws

Jennifer L. Manning-Paro. (2020, December). *Canine Front Limb Dewclaw Removal and the Resulting Carpal Injury and Arthritis Risks.* Hands of Grace Animal Massage and Bodywork. https://

www.handsofgraceanimalmassageandbodywork.com/blog/
canine-front-limb-dewclaw-removal-and-the-resulting-carpal-
injury-and-arthritis-risks

The Natural Dog - A Guide to Raw Diet and Health the Natural Way. (n.d.). Rawfed Dogs - The Natural Dog. http://rawfeddogs.org/rawguide

P. (2020, February 2). *A good article on dangerous things for our dogs to ingest.* Poodle Forum. https://www.poodleforum.com/threads/a-good-article-on-dangerous-things-for-our-dogs-to-ingest.185626/

Neff, Mark & Beck, John & Koeman, Julie & Boguslawski, Elissa & Kefene, Lisa & Borgman, Andrew & Ruhe, Alison. (2012). *Partial Deletion of the Sulfate Transporter SLC13A1 Is Associated with an Osteochondrodysplasia in the Miniature Poodle Breed.* PloS one. 7. e51917. 10.1371/journal.pone.0051917.

PetMD Editorial. (2016, April 7). *Degeneration of the Image Forming Part of the Eye in Dogs.* PetMD. https://www.petmd.com/dog/conditions/eyes/c_dg_retinal_degeneration

Pride & Prejudoodles. "What Do the Different Generations of Goldendoodles Mean?" *Pride & Prejudoodles*, Pride & Prejudoodles, https://www.prideandprejudoodles.com/blog/what-do-the-different-generations-of-goldendoodles-mean/

Made in the USA
Middletown, DE
21 December 2024

67993113R00097